Options Odyssey: Navigating the World of Trading Strategies

Unlocking Opportunities in the Stock Market

Michael Roberts

Table of Contents

INTRODUCTION

"Options Odyssey" embarks on an enlightening journey through the intricate landscape of options trading, guiding novice and experienced traders alike in mastering sophisticated trading strategies. This comprehensive guide illuminates the path to financial empowerment by exploring the fundamental concepts of options trading alongside an extensive range of techniques that can be tailored to any market condition or investment goal.

From the basics of calls and puts to the complexities of multi-leg strategies and hedging, this book equips you with the knowledge to navigate the volatile world of the stock market. Each chapter is meticulously crafted to ensure you grasp the essentials of options contracts and market dynamics.

"Options Odyssey" is not just a manual but a strategic partner in your trading career. It stands out by covering technical skills and fostering a deep understanding of market psychology and risk assessment. Maximize your potential in the stock market with our expert assistance. Our help—this indispensable resource is designed to turn ambitious traders into savvy market strategists.

CHAPTER I

Foundations of Options Trading

What are options and how do they work?

"Options Odyssey: Navigating the World of Trading Strategies" thoroughly examines options trading and gives readers a grasp of how options function within the context of sophisticated trading methods. Financial instruments known as options give the buyer the option—but not the obligation—to purchase or sell an underlying asset before a specific date at a given price. They are essential instruments in the financial markets, serving a variety of functions such as revenue production, hedging, and speculation.

The two primary forms of options are put and call options. The call option holder has a fixed period to purchase the asset at a predefined price. When the holder of this kind of option believes that the asset's price will climb and they will be able to buy it at a reduced price, they usually use it. A put option, on the other hand, is advantageous if the holder anticipates a decline in the asset's price, which will allow them to sell it at a higher price. The put option holder has the right to sell the asset at a predetermined price before the option's expiration.

The pricing of an option is affected by the underlying asset's current market price, the option's exercise price (strike price), the time value (period till expiration), and the underlying asset's volatility. The concepts of intrinsic worth and time value are essential among them. The difference between the asset's current price and the strike price is its inherent value, but only if it is positive. As the expiration date draws near, the time value decreases, which is a reflection of the declining probability that the price will move in the right direction.

In "Options Odyssey," options trading is depicted both on regulated exchanges and over-the-counter (OTC), where contracts can be tailored to the buyer and seller's particular requirements. Options are a crucial component of many financial strategies, especially risk management techniques, because of their flexibility. For example, an investor may use options to guard against possible losses in their stock holdings, or a corporation may use them as a hedge against changes in commodity prices that could have an impact on its operations.

Additionally, options-based speculative methods are covered in detail. These methods show how traders can leverage relatively small funds to get exposure to significant price changes in underlying assets. However, because these techniques rely so heavily on the ability to predict price movements precisely, they represent a higher risk of loss. The book also explores complex pricing models such as Black-Scholes, which assist traders in valuing options according to anticipated volatility and other market factors.

"Options Odyssey" also highlights the significance of comprehending "the Greeks," which are measurements that characterize how sensitive an option's price is to different factors. For instance, delta quantifies the predicted change in an option's price for every unit change in the cost of the underlying asset. Delta's rate of change is reflected in gamma. Theta is the pace at which, under all other circumstances, the cost of an option declines over time. Vega gauges volatility sensitivity, while Rho addresses interest rate fluctuations.

Institutional investors and organizations, as well as individual investors and speculators, employ options strategically for a variety of tactical financial goals. These can include anything from creating intricate financial instruments that provide novel approaches to risk management and investment to controlling foreign exchange exposure.

"Options Odyssey" delves into the regulatory structure that oversees the trading of options, emphasizing the significance of conforming to lawful norms and principled trading techniques. By doing this, investors are shielded from possible fraud and manipulation and the markets are kept fair and transparent.

By the end of the book, readers should have a theoretical understanding of choices and their applications and practical knowledge of how to apply options and methods in actual situations. The goal of the book is to turn inexperienced traders into knowledgeable market participants who can efficiently add options to their trading portfolios.

Through shedding light on the numerous ways options can improve trading strategies and risk management tactics and ultimately open up new chances in the stock market, "Options Odyssey" provides a thorough investigation into the world of options trading that not only teaches but also empowers investors. For traders of all skill levels, the detailed explanation demystifies a complicated subject, making it understandable and applicable.

Types of options: Calls and Puts

Through two main instruments, call options and put options, options trading, a sophisticated yet fascinating field of finance, gives investors the flexibility to achieve various financial goals, including income creation, hedging, and speculative profits. Anyone attempting to navigate this complex market must be aware of these solutions' differences and functionality.

Call option holders are not obligated to acquire an underlying asset (e.g., stocks, commodities, or indices) at the strike price.

However, they are free to do so. Call option buyers typically do so because they believe that before the option expires, the market value of the underlying asset will climb above the strike price. Buying a call is appealing because it allows you to control a large portion of the underlying asset with a comparatively small amount of capital, which might result in enormous rewards if the market moves in your favor. The call buyer could forfeit the entire option premium if the projected price increase is not realized.

In contrast, the holder of a put option may choose to sell the underlying asset at the strike price before the option expiration, but they are not obligated to. Typically, investors who buy put options do so because they think the underlying asset's price will soon drop below the strike price. This kind of option protects investors' equity positions from possible losses by acting like insurance. Speculative traders have a low-risk technique to profit from price declines using put options because they are identical to calls but can profit from dropping markets. Both call and put option prices are influenced by several variables, including the asset's present price, the strike price, the time value to expiration, and the underlying asset's volatility.

Time value and inherent value are important factors in price. The difference between the asset's current price and the strike price is, in essence, intrinsic value, but only if it is advantageous to the option holder. It represents the actual value that any option would have if it were exercised today. Time value is predicated on the possibility that the option's value will rise before expiration, mainly determined by the amount of time left and market volatility.

From small individual investors to major institutional traders, a wide range of market participants employ options which can be traded on exchanges or over the counter. There are many different call-and-put tactics. A straightforward approach is the "covered call," in which the investor sells a call option to earn money from the premium received while holding the underlying asset. Because the premium obtained can partially offset loss if the asset's price decreases, this method also offers a small hedge. On the other hand, a "protective put" entail purchasing a put option in addition to holding shares to hedge against a drop in the asset's value.

Combinations of purchasing and selling calls and puts, sometimes referred to as spreads, straddles, and strangles, are examples of advanced tactics that can be utilized to maximize profit from market moves in various situations. However, these tactics necessitate a deep comprehension of the fundamentals of options trading and market conditions.

Options are intricate financial tools with dangers, even with their tremendous return potential. Options' leverage effect has the potential to amplify both gains and losses. Therefore, they are only appropriate for some investors. To trade options profitably, one needs a well-honed risk management plan and a wealth of knowledge and expertise.

In conclusion, calls and puts are effective financial instruments that, when handled carefully, can strengthen an investor's portfolio by offering extra income, security, and speculation chances. Mastering these options entails using them strategically in line with one's investing objectives and risk tolerance, in addition to comprehending their pricing and market dynamics. Options trading's usefulness and complexity guarantee that it will always be a crucial subject for financial education and research, even as its appeal grows.

Components of an option contract: Strike price, expiration date, premium, etc.

A legally binding option contract grants the buyer the right—but not the responsibility—to buy or sell an underlying asset in the financial market on or before a specified date at a defined price. This contract's striking price, expiry date, and premium are the main factors that determine its value and suitability for an investor's strategy.

In any option contract, the striking price—also referred to as the exercise price—is an integral component. This price is the underlying asset's purchase price in the case of a call option and the selling price in the case of a put option. This price is fixed at contract creation and won't change until the option expires. The strike price is strategically chosen to represent the buyer's expectations and market projections. An investor might purchase a call option with a $110 strike price, for example, if they think a stock presently priced at $100 would increase to $120. The investor stands to profit from exercising the option if the stock price rises above this strike price before it expires.

An option's expiration date is when it loses its validity, and the ability to exercise it is forfeited. Though many standardized options expire on the third Friday of each month, choices may have a lifespan of days to years. One of the main factors influencing an option's premium is how long it has until expiration; generally, an option with a longer expiration date would have a greater premium. This is so that the underlying asset has more time to move favorably with a longer duration. For the option holder, who must choose between exercising the option, selling it, or letting it expire worthless, the expiration date is a crucial deadline.

The premium is the sum that the writer or seller of the option receives from the customer. This amount depends on a number of factors, including the strike price, the underlying asset's current price, the time till expiration, the asset's volatility, and the risk-free interest rate. In essence, the premium represents the cost of the rights granted by the option, taking into account both the time value—the additional value derived from the possibility that the option's value would rise before it expires—and any intrinsic value, if any. If the market value of the underlying asset exceeds the strike price, an investor can buy a call option with intrinsic value. The premium would only represent the underlying asset's time value and volatility if the market price was lower than the strike price.

Option contracts include additional details in addition to these main elements. These include the type of option

(American or European, which can only be exercised on the expiration date), contract size (the total number of shares or units of the asset covered by a single contract), and settlement method (cash settlement or physical delivery of the underlying asset). Each of these elements may have an impact on the option's financial result and strategic application.

Option contracts are used by investors as a hedge against possible losses, a way to bet on the volatility of the underlying asset, or a way to make money by collecting premiums. But trading options necessitates a deep comprehension of the market and its workings, as well as a thorough comprehension of how the three main elements—premium, expiration date, and strike price—interact and influence the overall investing plan. Options are best suited for seasoned investors who can handle the associated risks due to their complexity.

Traders and investors may more skillfully navigate the complexities of the options market and make well-informed choices that suit their risk tolerance and financial objectives when they have a thorough understanding of these components. Every element has a significant impact on the dynamics of options trading, affecting both the risks and possible profits. Having this knowledge is essential for developing strategies in the highly volatile financial markets that maximize profits or reduce losses.

Buying vs. selling options

In the world of options trading, one can choose to buy or sell options, and each method has advantages and disadvantages. For traders hoping to navigate this complicated market successfully, they must comprehend the ramifications of purchasing versus selling options.

By purchasing an option, a trader gains the right, for a predetermined length of time, to make a purchase at the strike price or sell the underlying asset. The premium is the price paid for this privilege. No matter how negatively the market goes, option buyers profit from a risk capped at the premium amount. Because of this, purchasing options are especially appealing for speculative investors or those looking to hedge against other financial positions. Purchasing a put option could reduce prospective losses by acting as an insurance policy against a decrease in the stock price. On the other hand, traders can profit from prospective stock price increases by purchasing a call option instead of making a significant investment in the stock itself.

When a trader sells or "writes" an option, they assume the risk that should the option buyer decide to exercise their right, they will have to purchase or sell the underlying asset. Typically, this tactic is used to make money from the premiums obtained from selling the options. The seller must fulfil the contract at the striking price, regardless of the market price. Hence, this strategy includes unlimited risk. For instance, a trader might have to sell an asset for substantially less than market value if they sell a call option and its value soars. Similarly, selling a put option carries some risk if the asset price drops considerably since the seller will have to pay more than the market value for the asset.

Selling options can be profitable, but it frequently depends on the assets staying mostly steady or moving in the seller's favor. Many seasoned traders use covered calls, where they sell call options and possess the underlying asset, to increase the income from their assets. Since the trader already possesses the asset they are required to sell, this strategy helps to reduce risk. The cash-secured put is another popular method in which a trader sells options on an item they want to possess in the hopes of either making money from the premium or getting the asset for less.

The trader's investing goals, risk tolerance, and market forecast should all be considered when deciding whether to purchase or sell options. Purchasing options allow investors to increase their capital exposure to potentially significant price movements without taking on a sizable financial risk. Conversely, sellers, especially in more unpredictable markets, are typically more interested in taking on greater risk to generate regular income through premium collection.

In order to purchase or sell options, the dynamics of the market must be well understood by traders and the particular elements that affect option pricing, such as volatility, time decay, and price fluctuations of the underlying asset. In addition, traders need to be skilled at controlling the risks related to the chosen methods, whether controlling possible infinite losses when selling options or restricting losses when purchasing them.

Additionally, traders must understand how time decay affects option prices. Because options are time-sensitive financial instruments, their value tends to decline as the expiration date draws near—a phenomenon called theta. This feature of options can be detrimental to buyers, particularly if the underlying asset's price moves against expectations. On the other hand, if other market conditions hold, theta can be advantageous to sellers, who frequently gain from the depreciation of the option's temporal value.

Purchasing and selling options are distinct techniques that meet various risk tolerances and trading goals. Purchasing options is a low-risk approach for investors with particular protection needs or a more cautious risk appetite to speculate on asset price changes or hedge current positions. Although selling options might be more profitable because premiums might be received, doing so demands a more significant risk tolerance and a well-thought-out plan to handle possibly limitless losses. Therefore, mastering options trading requires a solid understanding of option pricing mechanics and market fundamentals and a disciplined approach to risk management. With expertise, traders frequently discover that, depending on shifting market conditions and individual investment objectives, buying and selling techniques can be used to maximize their investment outcomes.

Overview of the options market

An essential part of the financial world, the options market presents a challenging but fascinating environment for traders and investors looking to optimize returns, manage risks, or speculate on financial instruments. A derivative contract known as an option grants its possessor the option—but not the obligation—to purchase the underlying asset or sell it at a fixed price before the contract's expiration. Because of its complexity and strategic opportunities, this market presents participants with challenges and rewards.

The two main categories of options are put (which offers the right to sell) and call (which gives the right to purchase). This dual character allows for various risk appetites and market perspectives, facilitating aggressive speculative plays and cautious hedging techniques. The market is driven by over the counter (OTC) transactions and regulated exchanges, each with unique features and a target market.

Options contracts are standardized about contract size, expiration, and striking price on regulated exchanges such as the Chicago Board Options Exchange (CBOE). This standardization makes it easier for many participants, including hedge funds, financial institutions, and ordinary traders, to participate and be liquid. Transparency, justice, and a lower risk of counterparties are guaranteed by the regulatory agencies that monitor trading on these exchanges, including the US Securities and Exchange Commission (SEC).

Conversely, participants can customize contracts on the OTC market concerning size, expiration date, and striking price. Compared to exchange-traded options, this customization has lesser liquidity and greater counterparty risk, but it also gives flexibility to suit specific demands or tactics. Usually, OTC transactions are limited to experienced or institutional investors who need particular solutions not offered by exchange-traded products.

The options market is a vital instrument for financial management, serving as more than just a place to trade. Businesses use options to hedge against changes in the prices of other assets, such as currencies and commodities, and portfolio managers use options to hedge against market or security downturns. While this carries a higher risk, speculators utilize options to wager on the direction of market prices without making the significant cash investment necessary to hold the underlying asset physically.

The underlying asset's current price, the option's strike price, the amount of time until expiration, the asset's volatility, and current interest rates all impact pricing in the options market, which is a complicated process. The Black-Scholes model, which offers theoretical prices for options based on these variables, is the most well-known model for pricing options. To effectively control the risks involved in options trading and make well-informed decisions, traders must comprehend and apply these pricing models.

The options market has risks and difficulties, though. Options' leverage effect has the potential to boost and magnify gains. Due to the market's complexity, a thorough grasp of financial systems and ongoing attention to market developments are necessary. 'Time decay', or the depreciation of an option's value as it gets closer to expiration, and the way implied volatility affects option pricing before important market events are among the things that traders need to be aware of.

Furthermore, the options market may be significantly impacted by changes in a particular industry as well as the overall state of the economy. Geopolitical events, policy changes, economic data releases, and earnings announcements can all lead to notable volatility, which offers traders both chances and hazards. Effectively navigating these waters necessitates a solid grasp of options and their inherent intricacies and skill in emotion control and trading discipline.

The market for options is essential to the global financial system by acting as a tool for risk management and price discovery. It provides a broad range of tactics, from cautious hedging to aggressive speculating, for traders and investors. Gaining expertise in this industry can be quite advantageous, but it calls for a solid foundation in knowledge, sharp analytical abilities, and strict risk management procedures. To thrive in options trading, participants must thus constantly learn new things and adjust to the volatile character of the financial markets.

How options are traded: Exchanges and OTC

Options trading is an intricate financial activity essential to contemporary markets. It allows investors to make predictions about market movements, protect their current holdings, or make money using various tactics. The two leading platforms used for this trading are OTC markets and regulated exchanges, each with unique features and catering to different investor needs.

Exchanges that are subject to regulation, such as the New York Stock Exchange (NYSE) and the Chicago Board Options Exchange (CBOE). The strike price, expiration date, and quantity of the underlying asset are just a few of the standardized contract terms, thanks to these exchanges. Standardization of this kind promotes liquidity and makes it easier for investors to locate counterparties for their trades.

The lower counterparty risk is one of the main advantages of trading on an exchange. A clearinghouse, which serves as the counterparty to both parties in a transaction, reduces this risk. The clearinghouse contributes to the preservation of market integrity and confidence by ensuring the fulfilment of all contracts. Moreover, regulatory agencies that uphold laws intended to safeguard investors and preserve equitable trading conditions supervise exchanges, like the Securities and Exchange Commission (SEC) in the United States.

Market makers are essential to these exchanges because they maintain the bid and ask prices for options and are prepared to purchase or sell at these prices, providing liquidity. By reducing bid-ask spreads, this activity makes the market more fluid and facilitates more efficient transaction execution by other market players.

OTC markets provide a more flexible trading environment where parties can directly negotiate contract terms with one other, in contrast to the heavily controlled exchange environment. Because of this versatility, contract sizes, expiration dates, and strike prices can all be customized to meet unique requirements or intricate strategies that may not be possible with ordinary exchange-traded options.

Large institutional investors who seek customized solutions for their hedging or investment needs are the primary users of OTC options. For instance, a multinational company can use OTC options to precisely match the risk profile of its expected international earnings when hedging currency exposure.

However, the flexibility of the OTC market has drawbacks, such as increased counterparty risk and less transparency. There is an inherent risk of default in the OTC market since prices are not publicly disclosed, and each party depends on the other's creditworthiness and capacity to fulfil contractual obligations. OTC transaction participants frequently use collateral agreements and credit derivatives to control this risk and guard against counterparty defaults.

The investor's demands significantly influence whether to trade on an exchange or in the OTC market. Small institutions and individual investors may favor regulated markets due to their uniformity, accessibility, and seeming security. They can take advantage of the transparent pricing, reduced counterparty risk, and simplicity of entering and leaving trades here.

On the other hand, significant institutions and knowledgeable investors may prefer the OTC market due to its flexibility in customizing contracts to meet specific needs. Although this market has more flexibility, there is also more danger involved, and you must have the financial resources to cover losses.

Investors must thoroughly understand how options function, including how time decay, volatility, and movements in underlying assets affect pricing dynamics, to trade well in either market. Additionally, it's critical to possess a thorough understanding of both market types' operational mechanisms and regulatory frameworks. With this information, investors may make well-informed selections that complement their investment philosophies and risk appetites.

In conclusion, options trading on exchanges and in over-the-counter (OTC) markets is essential to the financial system because it provides income production, risk management, and speculation instruments. Since each trading platform serves a distinct market niche, it has a unique combination of benefits and drawbacks. By being aware of the subtleties of these platforms, investors can more successfully accomplish their financial goals and traverse the complicated world of options trading.

Economic indicators and their impact on options

Economic indicators are vital in the financial markets because they affect investor sentiment and asset prices, including option values. These metrics show the state of a nation or region's economy and include information on employment, inflation, GDP growth, and consumer confidence, among other things. It is crucial for traders who want to profit from or protect themselves from economic swings to comprehend how these indicators impact options trading.

First, GDP growth, which gauges a nation's total economic production, is one of the most closely followed economic metrics. A healthy economy is indicated by solid GDP growth, which can raise investor confidence and drive up stock values. This could result in an increase in call option prices for options traders as the underlying stocks gain value. On the other hand, if GDP growth is less rapid than anticipated, stock prices may fall, which would raise the value of put options as investors look to hedge against weakening markets.

Another important economic indicator is inflation, especially in light of its effect on central banks' control over interest rates. In reaction to growing inflation, interest rates rise, which can stifle economic expansion and stock market gains. Higher interest rates may have the effect of decreasing the present value of stocks for options traders. This might lead to a fall in call option prices but an increase in put option prices because of the increased risk of stock price declines.

The mood of the market is also greatly influenced by employment data, such as non-farm payrolls and unemployment rates. Stronger economic growth and increased consumer spending are typically the results of high employment, and these factors can support call options as well as the stock market. Conversely, growing joblessness can undermine consumer confidence and spending, harming business earnings and stock values. As a result, investors may seek refuge, which could increase the value of put options.

Consumer confidence indexes reveal a consumer's level of optimism or pessimism about their financial future, which directly affects their purchase decisions. Since strong consumer confidence indicates increased spending and a thriving economy, higher stock values are generally supported by it. As a result, rising consumer confidence may result in higher call option prices while lowering put option attraction.

The interest rates have significant influence since they are directly determined by central banks. Lower interest rates lower borrowing costs, which could encourage capital spending and strengthen stock markets. In general, this is a favorable environment for call options. On the other hand, when borrowing prices rise in response to rising interest rates, there's a chance that investment and stock market performance may decline, which could lead to an increase in put options.

To assess the state of the manufacturing industry, traders also keep an eye on manufacturing data, such as the Purchasing Managers' Index (PMI). A strong manufacturing sector is indicative of a strong economy and can lead to bullish stock markets, which is good news for call options. On the other hand, a falling PMI may indicate impending economic problems, which might increase the value of put options as investors brace for declines.

But market expectations also play a mediating role in how economic indicators affect options. Markets are frequently moved by how economic data compares to expectations rather than the actual economic data release.

For example, even if the data only reveals a slight improvement, markets may respond favorably if it exceeds market expectations. On the other hand, markets might respond badly if data doesn't match expectations. For options traders, who must accurately assess both the direction and strength of market movements in order to efficiently manage their holdings, this disparity is critical.

Furthermore, the peculiarities of options—such as their susceptibility to fluctuations in market volatility, symbolized by the Greek letter "Vega"—also influence how economic data affect the way they are priced. For example, options with greater volatility are typically more expensive since there is a greater chance of large price fluctuations and in-the-money outcomes.

To sum up, economic indicators are crucial instruments for options traders since they offer insights into the future trends and attitudes of the market. Traders may make better selections about which options to purchase or sell by keeping a close eye on these indicators and predicting how changes in the economy may affect various industries and asset classes. This information is vital for controlling risk in a portfolio as well as for making predictions about future movements. It also enables traders to position themselves favorably in a range of economic situations. An essential skill in the toolbox of a profitable options trader is therefore the ability to comprehend and respond to economic indications.

Company fundamentals: Earnings, dividends, and news releases

In the ever-changing world of finance, investors looking to make well-informed judgments must have a solid understanding of a company's core values. Three essential elements stand out in this context: press announcements, earnings, and dividends. Earnings are usually reported quarterly or annually and show the company's financial performance over a period. They indicate profitability, showing how well the business can raise money and control costs. A company that is growing and doing well is usually indicated by positive earnings growth, which draws in investors looking for possible profits. On the other hand, diminishing or negative profits could make investors question the company's financial stability and prospects in the future.

Conversely, dividends are payments made to shareholders from a company's profits. They act as an incentive, giving a portion of the company's earnings to investors who contribute funds. Investors, particularly those looking for income-oriented investments, can receive a consistent income stream via dividends.

Income-seeking investors view companies with a history of stable and growing dividends favorably because they show financial stability and confidence in future earnings. Dividend payments can also indicate management's commitment to long-term sustainability and shareholder value.

An essential factor in influencing investor perceptions and market mood is news releases. Press releases, earnings announcements, and other business updates are some of the ways that companies frequently keep the financial community and shareholders informed. Through these communications, the company's performance, strategic goals, and prospects for the future are all made clear. Good news releases can boost investor confidence and cause stock prices to rise. Examples of these announcements include impressive earnings reports or noteworthy corporate advances. On the other hand, unfavorable information, such as missed results or problems with regulations, can lead to selling pressure and a drop in stock prices.

The complex and dynamic relationship between news releases, dividends, and earnings affects market patterns and investor behavior. Robust profit growth has the potential to enhance investor confidence and facilitate dividend hikes, thereby gratifying shareholders and drawing in new capital. Positive press releases can intensify this effect, strengthening the story of a business that is both successful and promising. On the other hand, unsatisfactory results or bad news can undermine investor confidence, resulting in dividend reductions or suspension and forcing shareholders to reconsider their investing philosophy.

Investors obtain information from various sources to stay current on company fundamentals. A company's financial statements, which include income statements, balance sheets, and cash flow statements, thoroughly reveal its financial performance and condition. Industry publications, regulatory filings, and analyst reports are additional sources of insightful viewpoints and analysis. In addition, investors keep a close eye on social media, financial websites, and news sources for real-time information and market discussion.

Analyzing corporate fundamentals requires a balanced approach that considers both quantitative and qualitative aspects. News releases offer subjective insights into the company's strategic direction and competitive landscape, while earnings and dividends provide objective indicators of financial performance. Investors must consider these aspects in light of industry dynamics, competitive pressures, and broader economic developments. Making wise investment selections also requires understanding the connection between stock pricing and company fundamentals.

To sum up, market dynamics and investor views are influenced by various elements included in company fundamentals. News releases, dividends, and earnings are essential measures of a company's performance, financial health, and future prospects. By comprehending and evaluating these basics, investors can manage the complexity of the financial markets and make well-informed judgments. A deep comprehension of business principles is necessary for long-term investment success, regardless of whether one is looking for growth prospects or income-producing investments.

Chart patterns and technical indicators

Technical analysis is a potent technique utilized in the financial markets by traders and investors to estimate future price movements by analyzing historical market data. Chart patterns and technical indicators, which provide insightful information about market trends, momentum, and possible turning moments, are the foundation of technical analysis. Head and shoulders, triangles, and double tops and bottoms are examples of recurrent forms on price charts that indicate possible changes in the mood and direction of the market. These patterns, which are frequently accompanied by specific price and volume features, are created by the aggregate action of market participants. Traders can predict future price changes and adjust their trading methods by identifying and analyzing these patterns.

Technical indicators give quantifiable measurements of price movements and market conditions, complementing chart patterns. These indicators are computed mathematically using volume, price history, or a combination. Moving averages, the relative strength index (RSI), stochastic oscillators, and MACD (moving average convergence divergence) are common technical indicators. For example, moving averages smooth price data to reveal trends and levels of support and resistance. Price changes' momentum is determined by the RSI and stochastic oscillator, which show overbought or oversold circumstances. Conversely, moving averages are combined by MACD to indicate shifts in trend momentum.

The capacity of chart patterns and technical indicators to depict the psychology and behavior of the market accounts for their efficacy. The tug-of-war between buyers and sellers is reflected in chart patterns like trendlines and support/resistance levels, which show how supply and demand are balanced in the market.

Breakouts from these patterns indicate a change in the market dynamics, which frequently results in significant price moves. Likewise, technical indicators aid traders in determining possible entry and exit situations by offering perceptions of the underlying strength or weakness of price patterns. Traders can combine technical indicators and chart patterns to formulate an approach to trading that accounts for both price movement and market sentiment.

It is imperative to acknowledge the constraints of technical analysis and the associated hazards. Technical indicators and chart patterns can provide insightful information about market trends but are not infallible predictions of future price moves. Technical signals may be superseded by various factors that impact market dynamics, such as economic data, geopolitical developments, and investor sentiment. In addition, traders may disagree because technical analysis is subjective and open to different interpretations. Because of this, traders must use prudence and integrate risk management tactics into their trading plans.

There are many different financial markets where technical indicators and chart patterns are used, including equities, currencies, commodities, and cryptocurrencies. Since every market has its peculiarities and patterns of activity, trading strategies must be flexible and adaptive. In addition, the development of algorithmic trading and quantitative analysis has facilitated the emergence of automated trading systems that employ technical indicators and chart patterns to execute trades efficiently. To find patterns and signals in massive volumes of market data, these systems use sophisticated statistical models and machine learning algorithms. This allows for quick decision-making and execution.

To sum up, technical indicators and chart patterns are invaluable resources for traders and investors trying to make their way through the intricacies of the financial markets. Traders can obtain important insights into market trends, momentum, and possible turning moments by comprehending and analyzing these patterns and signals. But it's crucial to approach technical analysis with a critical mindset and support it with risk management strategies and fundamental analysis.

Finding the right balance between objectivity and intuition is ultimately what makes technical analysis an art form, allowing traders to use data and analysis to make well-informed judgments.

Using technical analysis to predict option price movements

Within the financial markets, options trading provides traders and investors with a flexible means of controlling risk and making profits. Although many variables affect the price of options, such as time decay, volatility, and underlying asset values, technical analysis offers a valuable framework for forecasting option movements. Technical analysis examines historical market data, including volume and price, to find patterns and trends that are predictive of future changes in price. By utilizing technical analysis techniques, trading options can provide traders with insights into possible price direction, volatility shifts, and best times to enter and exit the market.

Examining underlying asset price movements is one of the core ideas of technical analysis as it relates to options trading. The price changes of the underlying asset directly affect how much options cost. Therefore, traders can determine the direction of the underlying asset's price and predict corresponding moves in the price of options by examining price charts and spotting trends using tools like moving averages, trendlines, and support/resistance levels. For instance, higher option prices may result from increased demand for call options during a strong upswing in the stock market. On the other hand, put options may gain value during a decline and see a price increase.

Because it represents the size of price swings in the underlying asset, volatility is a critical factor in the pricing of options. To quantify and examine volatility levels, technical analysis provides a number of indicators, including Bollinger Bands, Average True Range (ATR), and historical volatility. Traders can predict possible changes in options pricing brought on by changes in market mood and expectations for volatility by keeping an eye on trends and patterns in volatility. For example, as traders anticipate greater price fluctuations, rising volatility frequently results in higher option premiums. On the other hand, when uncertainty decreases, decreasing volatility can lead to reduced option pricing.

Another important source of information about changes in options prices is chart patterns. Options pricing may be impacted by patterns like triangles, flags, and pennants, which can indicate possible breakout or breakdown scenarios. Chart pattern breakouts frequently correspond with higher trading volume and volatility, giving options traders the chance to profit from price momentum. Technical indicators that confirm the strength of market moves and identify overbought or oversold conditions, which may affect options pricing, include the MACD, or moving average convergence divergence, and the RSI, or relative strength index.

Technical analysis can also be used by option traders to determine the best times to enter and exit trades. Technical indicators, chart patterns, and trend analysis can all be used by traders to create trading strategies that minimize risk and optimize possible gains. To identify possible trend reversals, traders would, for instance, search for divergence between price and momentum indicators. This would enable them to enter or exit positions at advantageous price points.

Technical analysis-identified levels of support and resistance can also be important junctures to use when deciding whether to place stop-loss orders or set profit objectives. It's crucial to recognize that technical analysis has limitations when it comes to forecasting changes in option prices. Technical analysis alone may not be sufficient to adequately capture the effects of time decay (theta), interest rates, and changes in implied volatility (Vega) on options pricing. To make wise trading decisions, traders should therefore combine technical analysis with fundamental analysis and a working knowledge of options Greeks.

To sum up, technical analysis offers an effective framework for forecasting changes in option prices and spotting trading opportunities in the options market. Traders can obtain important insights about possible price direction and the best times to enter and exit option trades by examining underlying asset price trends, volatility patterns, and chart formations. To make better decisions, one must be aware of the limitations of technical analysis and take into account additional elements like fundamental analysis and options Greeks. In the end, navigating the intricacies of the options market takes a thorough approach that incorporates a variety of analytical tools and tactics for effective options trading.

CHAPTER II

Options Trading Strategies

Long Call and Long Put

Investors and traders in the derivatives market utilize two primary strategies—long call and long put options—to provide predictions about the movement of the underlying asset prices. These techniques present unique profit and risk management chances, contingent upon investment goals and market conditions. The holder of a long call option has the opportunity, but not the duty, to purchase the to buy the underlying asset during the specified window (the option's expiration date) at the strike price. This tactic is used when an investor anticipates a substantial increase in the cost underlying asset's price, enabling them to profit from the asset's value growth. With a relatively small initial investment, the investor can purchase a long call option, increasing their influence over the underlying asset and limiting their exposure to downside risk to the option's premium.

On the other hand, a long-put option gives its holder the choice—but not the duty—to execute a fixed-price sale of the underlying asset (the strike price). within a given window (the expiration date). When investors believe that the cost underlying an asset's price will significantly decrease, they employ the long-put strategy. Purchasing a long-put option allows an investor to profit from a drop in the asset's price by capping potential losses at the option's premium. By offering insurance against unfavorable price fluctuations, investors can use this strategy to hedge against downside risk or speculate on potential market downturns in the future.

Compared to outright ownership of the underlying asset, long call and extended put options provide leverage, enabling investors to hold a more significant position with a lower initial investment. It's crucial to remember that leverage increases possible profits and losses, making options trading fundamentally riskier than regular stock trading. Therefore, before using options trading methods, investors should thoroughly consider their investing goals and risk tolerance.

The length of time before expiration, implied volatility fluctuations, and the size of price moves in the underlying asset are some variables that affect how profitable long call and long put options are. When the underlying asset's value climbs above the strike price of a long call option, the holder of the option may exercise it to purchase the asset at a a discount to its market value, making the option more profitable. On the other hand, long-put options become more profitable when the underlying asset's price drops below the strike price, allowing the option holder to sell the item for more than its market value.

The value of long call and long put options is also affected by changes in implied volatility (Vega) and time decay (theta) in addition to price movements. Options' time value diminishes as they approach expiration, which could result in losses for option holders if the price of the underlying asset does not move in the expected direction. As a result, while trading long calls and extended put options, investors need to consider how time decay affects options pricing, making timing extremely important.

Moreover, implied volatility variations can impact the worth of options, incredibly long put options. Long-put option investors profit from increased options premiums due to increased implied volatility, which raises the value of their positions. On the other hand, a drop in implied volatility could lead to a reduction in option premiums, making long-put options less profitable.

To sum up, long-call and long-put options are flexible investment strategies that let investors profit from shifts in the underlying asset price. These tactics are appealing substitutes for conventional stock trading since they provide leverage and little danger of loss. However, there are inherent risks associated with options trading, such as implied volatility changes and time decay, which can affect how profitable long call and long put options are. Therefore, before implementing options trading techniques, investors should carefully consider the state of the market, their level of risk tolerance, and their investment goals.

Covered Call and Protective Put

Investors utilize covered calls and protective puts, two well-liked options trading techniques, to increase portfolio returns, control risk, and provide income. These techniques combine options contracts with underlying assets to accomplish specific investing goals while reducing downside risk. Writing (selling) call options on the same asset while maintaining a long position in the underlying asset is a covered call strategy. Selling the call options generates a premium for the investor, which helps defray any losses in the underlying asset and provides income. The revenue gained from the call premiums helps offset the possible adverse risk associated with a covered call strategy, with the maximum profit being restricted to the premium collected from selling the call options.

Conversely, a defensive put strategy entails buying put options on the same asset while maintaining a long position in the underlying asset. By enabling the investor to realize a predefined profit on the sale of the underlying asset (the strike price) within a given time frame (the expiration date), options serve as insurance against possible downside risk. Put options are purchased by the investor at a premium; this protects against unfavorable price changes in the underlying asset. The protective put strategy limits potential losses in the underlying asset and offers downside protection despite its upfront fees in the form of option premiums.

Investors can choose between specific benefits and trade-offs with covered call and defensive put strategies. Investors looking to earn income from their portfolio holdings and with reasonable bullishness on the underlying asset are good candidates for a covered call strategy. Investors can increase portfolio returns through option premiums while holding onto ownership of the underlying asset by selling call options against their current positions. However, the downside risk associated with a covered call strategy is that the commitment to sell the underlying asset at the call options' strike price may restrict possible gains from the asset's price growth. Conversely, investors worried about possible downside risk in their portfolio holdings can consider a protective put approach. Investors can safeguard the value of their portfolio by hedging against unfavorable price changes in the underlying asset by purchasing put options. The protection offered by puts helps prevent substantial losses in the case of a market downturn, even while the upfront cost of buying puts lowers total portfolio returns. Furthermore, investors can customize their hedging strategies according to their investment goals and risk tolerance thanks to the flexibility of put options.

Considering market conditions, such as volatility, time decay, and underlying asset price fluctuations, is necessary for covered call and protected put strategies. These strategies' performance is contingent on several variables, including the extent of price moves in the underlying asset, variations in implied volatility, and the time to expiration. Therefore, investors should undertake a comprehensive study and risk assessment before using covered call or protected put strategies in their portfolios.

In summary, investors can benefit from income production and risk control through the flexible options trading strategies of covered calls and protective puts. By integrating options contracts with underlying assets, investors can customize their investment approaches to leverage market opportunities while reducing the risk of negative returns. Before taking on covered calls or protective put bets, investors must carefully consider their risk tolerance, financial goals, and the trade-offs associated with these techniques. In the ever-changing world of options trading, covered call and protective put strategies can reduce downside risk and optimize portfolio returns when executed properly.

Spreads: Bull Spread, Bear Spread, Calendar Spread, Diagonal Spread

Investors utilize a wide variety of trading strategies known as spread options strategies to take advantage of market trends, control risk, and optimize portfolio returns. The calendar, diagonal, bear, and bull spread are the four most used spread techniques. A bull spread is a strategy in which a lower strike call option is bought and a higher strike call option is simultaneously sold on the identical expiration date and underlying asset. When an investor anticipates a moderate gain in the cost of the underlying asset, they will utilize this technique. Investors can restrict their initial outlay of funds while still having the chance to benefit if the underlying asset's price moves above the higher strike price by using a bull spread. A bull spread has a maximum profit cap and a maximum loss equal to the spread's initial premium.

However, you are using a bear spread strategy if you exchange one put option for another with a lower strike price and purchase one identical underlying asset strike price and expiration date. When an investor anticipates a slight decline in the cost underlying asset's price, they will employ this technique. Using a bear spread, investors can profit from downward market fluctuations while lowering their initial investment and potential losses. As with a bull spread, a bear spread has a maximum profit cap and a maximum loss equal to the spread's original premium. Purchasing and selling options on the same underlying asset and strike price with varying expiration dates is known as a calendar spread strategy. A calendar spread is typically put together by purchasing a longer-term option and concurrently selling a shorter-term option with the same strike price. When investors predict modest short-term price volatility but significant long-term price movement, they use this method. Investors can profit from the difference in time decay between the two options while limiting their exposure to risk by using calendar spread. The maximum loss on a calendar spread is capped at the spread's original premium, and the most significant profit is realized if the underlying asset's price is close to the strike price when the shorter-term option expires.

Finally, purchasing and selling options on the same underlying asset with varying strike prices and expiration dates is known as a diagonal spread strategy. A diagonal spread is created utilizing options with distinct strike prices instead of a calendar spread. When investors expect both price movement and time decay to go in their favor and have a directional bias on the underlying asset, they will use this technique. Investors can profit from the difference in time decay between the two options and the underlying asset's price movement by employing a diagonal spread. A diagonal spread's most significant profit and loss potential depends on several variables, such as the underlying asset's volatility and price movement.

To sum up, investors can achieve specific investment goals and navigate various market conditions with the help of spread options techniques. Investors may use spread techniques to take advantage of market changes, control risk, and improve portfolio returns, regardless of their attitude toward the underlying asset: optimistic, bearish, or neutral. However, before incorporating spread strategies into their portfolios, investors must be aware of the unique qualities and hazards connected with each one. Spread options techniques can be helpful tools for navigating the ever-changing financial markets with careful analysis and risk management.

Straddles and Strangles

Two sophisticated options trading methods investors use to profit from notable price swings in the underlying asset are strangles and straddles. The techniques differ in terms of expiration dates and strike prices, but both involve purchasing a call and a put option on the same underlying asset. Straddling is the practice of purchasing a call and a put option with the same dates of expiration and strike prices. Investors will use this strategy when they expect the underlying asset to see significant price volatility but are unsure of the direction of price movement. Investors can profit from significant price swings in either direction by using a straddle, provided the movement's magnitude surpasses the total premiums paid for the call-and-put options. In the case of a substantial price movement in either direction, the most significant profit potential from a straddle is theoretically unlimited. Still, the maximum loss is constrained to the initial premium paid for the options.

Alternatively, you might purchase a put and a call option that has the same expiration date but different strike prices by using a strangle method. Specifically, purchasing both an out-of-the-money call and put option on the same underlying asset is a common strangle technique. When investors believe that the price movement will be biased in one direction but still expect significant price volatility in the underlying asset, they will use this approach. Investors can profit from significant price swings in either direction using a strangle, but the approach is skewed in favor of the side with the higher strike price option. The maximum profit potential from a strangle is unlimited if the underlying asset has a significant price movement in the expected direction. Still, the maximum loss from the strategy is restricted to the original premium paid for the options.

Investors have access to a flexible toolkit with both straddles and strangles to help them navigate erratic market circumstances and profit from noteworthy price swings in the underlying asset. These are especially helpful when anticipating market-moving events with unknown outcomes, such as regulatory decisions, earnings announcements, or other occurrences. Investors can profit from volatility expansions while restricting their downside risk to the initial premium paid for the options using straddles and strangles. Nevertheless, because these methods depend on large price swings to produce gains, investors must pay close attention to the timing and size of market changes when putting them into practice.

It's also critical to be aware of the possible negative aspects of strangles and straddles, such as the influence of implied volatility fluctuations and time decay. Buying options, which experience time decay (theta) as their expiration date draws near, is a component of both strategies. To prevent significant losses, investors should be aware of how time decay affects the value of their options contracts and consider liquidating their holdings before expiration. Furthermore, implied volatility (Vega) variations can impact the worth of options, especially for strategies that profit from volatility expansions like straddles and strangles. Therefore, to optimize possible profits and efficiently manage risk, investors need to keep an eye on implied volatility changes and modify their positions as necessary.

To sum up, straddles and strangles are effective options trading techniques that allow investors to profit from notable price swings in erratic market environments. Investors can benefit from volatility expansions while limiting their downside risk to the initial premium paid for the options by buying both calls and putting options on the same underlying asset. When employing these methods, investors must pay close attention to the timing, size, and direction of price swings. They also need to know how time decay and variations in implied volatility may affect their options positions. Straddles and strangles can be valuable instruments for managing volatile financial markets with careful analysis and risk management.

Options Greeks: Delta, Gamma, Theta, Vega, Rho

How responsive the price of an option is to shifts in several variables, such as the cost of the underlying asset, time decay, volatility, interest rates, and dividend yields, is measured by a set of parameters called options Greeks. Investors can better comprehend and control the risks involved in options trading using Greek letters, each of which stands for a distinct facet of an option's price behavior. Delta, which indicates the rate at which the price of an option varies about changes in the underlying asset's price, is the most well-known and frequently used Options in Greek. A call option's delta, which shows the likelihood that the option will expire in-the-money, ranges typically from 0 to 1. The option's price will vary by about half as much as the underlying asset's price if the delta is 0.5. On the other hand, a put option has a delta that ranges from -1 to 0, where the option's price will move in the opposite direction by roughly half as much as the price of the underlying asset if the delta is -0.5.

Gamma expresses how quickly the delta of an option varies about shifts in the underlying asset's price. Gamma lowers as options move further into or out of the money and is highest for at-the-money options. Gamma is most sensitive to fluctuations in the underlying asset's price as expiration draws near; therefore, it is highest when an option is almost about to expire. Theta calculates the pace at which the cost of an option decays over time as expiration draws near. Theta falls as options move farther into or out of the money and is most excellent for at-the-money options. Theta increases in response to the increasing rate of time decay in the option's price as expiration draws near, which happens as options approach expiration.

The Vega indicator shows how sensitive an option's price is to variations in implied volatility. When an option moves farther into or out of the money, Vega falls from its maximum value for at-the-money options. Because of the option's increasing price sensitivity to changes in implied volatility as expiration draws near, Vega is highest when an option is almost ready to expire. Rho calculates how responsive the price of an option is to shifts in interest rates. Options with longer expiration dates and higher strike prices have the largest Rho. When interest rates rise, call options often see an increase in value, while put options see a reduction in value. Rho is usually positive for call options and negative for put options. However, other factors, including the cost of the underlying asset, volatility, and time decay, tend to possess a greater influence on option pricing than do interest rates.

For traders and investors to make wise choices and successfully manage risk in options trading, they must understand options Greeks. By examining the Greeks of their holdings, investors can assess the potential impact of fluctuations in interest rates, time decay, volatility, and the price of the underlying asset on their options contracts. Additionally, investors can create and modify their options strategies using Options Greeks to meet particular risk-return profiles and investment goals. Although Options Greeks offer insightful analysis of how options prices behave, investors must understand that they are theoretical models and may not accurately forecast actual price changes in the options market.

As a result, investors ought to employ Options Greeks in conjunction with other elements like technical and fundamental analysis as part of an all-encompassing risk management approach. Options Greeks can be effective instruments for navigating the intricacies of the options market and attaining long-term financial success if they are correctly understood and applied.

Volatility trading: Understanding implied and historical volatility

Analyzing and exploiting price swings in financial markets is the core activity of volatility trading. Implied volatility and historical volatility are two fundamental ideas in volatility trading. An asset's implied volatility denotes the market's expectations regarding its future price changes over a given time frame. It is calculated from the values of options contracts, representing the opinion of market players on the possible size of future price fluctuations. When there is uncertainty or market turbulence, implied volatility typically rises, and when there is stability or complacency, it usually falls. Traders apply tactics to profit from anticipated changes in volatility levels, using implied volatility as a gauge of market sentiment and uncertainty.

Historical volatility, on the other hand, gauges an asset's fundamental price changes over a given time frame. It offers insights into the asset's previous volatility patterns and behavior and is computed using historical price data. One might look at historical volatility to evaluate the state of the market today and contrast it with historical averages. Traders look to historical volatility data to determine the relative level of market volatility and spot trading opportunities. By examining past volatility patterns, traders can predict future shifts in the market dynamics and modify their trading tactics accordingly.

Implied and historical volatility are two different but closely connected ideas in volatility trading. While historical volatility indicates previous price movements, implied volatility is the market's forward-looking forecast of future price changes. Differences between implied and historical volatility can offer trading opportunities for wise traders. Inferred volatility may suggest that options are expensive compared to previous price movements if they are noticeably higher than historical volatility. In this situation, traders can think about selling options to profit on the volatility mean reversion—the difference between implied and actual volatility. On the other hand, if implied volatility is much lower than historical volatility, it can hint that options are cheap compared to previous price moves. If traders want to profit from future increases in volatility, they can think about purchasing options.

A wide variety of tactics are included in volatility trading, which aims to make money off variations in volatility levels. Positions taken by the anticipated direction of future volatility are known as directional volatility strategies. Volatility breakout methods, for instance, entail purchasing options when volatility rises over predetermined thresholds in anticipation of additional price swings in the same direction. Volatility arbitrage is one example of a non-directional volatility strategy that aims to take advantage of price differences between an options contract and the underlying asset. These techniques aim to make money on relative mispricing in volatility levels, independent of future price changes. Furthermore, options, futures, exchange-traded funds (ETFs), and other derivative instruments can be used with volatility trading tactics to offer traders flexibility and diversification.

Risk management is critical in volatility trading since market dynamics are inherently complicated and unpredictable. To reduce possible losses and protect cash, traders must carefully evaluate their risk tolerance, position size, and portfolio diversification. Hedging techniques, position limits, and stop-loss orders can all be used to control risk exposure and guard against unfavorable market moves. Furthermore, to limit possible losses and adjust to shifting market conditions, trading positions must be continuously monitored and adjusted. In the turbulent world of financial markets, traders can improve their prospects of long-term success and sustainability by implementing robust risk management procedures into their volatility trading methods.

To sum up, volatility trading is an active and diverse strategy for making money from changes in financial market prices. Essential ideas in volatility trading are implied volatility and historical volatility, which stand for historical price movements and market expectations. Traders use these measures to determine trading opportunities, assess market mood, and efficiently manage risk. Traders may effectively manage the intricacies of volatility trading and take advantage of market opportunities by comprehending the relationship between implied and historical volatility and utilizing suitable trading tactics. Volatility trading calls for perseverance, dedication, and ongoing education to consistently turn a profit and adjust to changing market conditions. With the right research, risk management, and execution, volatility trading can be a lucrative endeavor for traders hoping to profit on the inherent uncertainty and volatility of financial markets.

Writing covered calls for income

One common options trading tactic individuals use to profit from their current stock holdings is writing covered calls. Selling call options on stocks investors already hold is a covered call strategy. A contract for a call option represents one hundred shares of the underlying stock. Selling call options allows investors to earn premiums instantly. The investor forfeits the premium and if the buyer exercises the option before it expires, the seller is required to sell the underlying shares at the agreed-upon strike price.

When the underlying stock is anticipated to stay mostly constant or see minor price growth in neutral or mildly positive markets, writing covered calls can be a valuable strategy for increasing portfolio returns.

The main objective of writing the covered calls is to earn money from the premiums paid while holding onto the underlying stock. In addition to dividends from stock holdings, the income from writing covered calls can provide investors with a consistent flow of cash. Furthermore, as the premiums received lower the net cost basis of the stock position, writing covered calls may also lower the underlying stock's breakeven price in the case that the stock price declines, this can protect against losses and increase the overall return on investment.

The flexibility to tailor the strategy to the investor's risk tolerance and investing goals is a significant benefit of writing covered calls. Investors can select expiration dates and strike prices based on how they anticipate the price movement of the underlying stock. To generate income and keep a safety net against future losses, conservative investors may sell covered options with strike prices that are somewhat above the stock's current market price. These calls are referred to as out-of-the-money (OTM) calls. To maximize premium income, aggressive investors may opt to sell covered calls with strike prices that are in-the-money (ITM) or closer to the stock's current market price. This approach has a higher risk of the stock being called away.

When selling covered calls, risk management is crucial because the buyer's execution of the option could result in the underlying stock being called away. Investors can use several techniques, such as rolling options contracts, establishing profit targets, and putting stop-loss orders in place, to reduce this risk. Rolling options contracts entail closing current covered call positions and opening new ones simultaneously, but with different expiration dates or strike prices. This enables investors to modify their exposure to variations in the price and volatility of the underlying asset. Choosing the prices at which to purchase back the covered calls in order to achieve gains and exit the position is known as setting profit objectives.

Stop-loss orders can be used to restrict possible losses by automatically terminating covered call positions in the event that the underlying stock price drops below a predefined threshold.

Investors should be aware of the tax ramifications of writing covered calls since, depending on how long the underlying stock is held, premium income is usually either short-term or long-term capital gains. The opportunity cost of writing covered calls should also be considered by investors, as doing so eliminates their chance to profit infinitely in the event that the underlying stock appreciates significantly in value. Writing covered calls, however, can be a useful tactic to take into consideration for investors looking to manage downside risk while generating income from their stock holdings.

To sum up, covered call writing is a flexible options trading method that gives investors the chance to profit from the stocks they already own. Investors can profit while holding onto their underlying stocks by selling call options on stocks they already own. In sideways or slightly bullish markets, writing covered calls can insulate investors from downside volatility, increase portfolio returns, and give a consistent income stream. To reduce possible losses, investors must, however, be aware of the benefits and hazards of this strategy and have strong risk management procedures in place. For investors looking to take advantage of the advantages of options trading, writing covered calls can be a useful income-generating strategy with the right research, execution, and risk management.

Selling cash-secured puts

A practical options trading strategy investors use to make money or buy the stock at a specific price is selling cash-secured puts. By selling put options on companies they are willing to own, investors can profit from this technique. A contract for a put option represents one hundred shares of the underlying stock. "Cash-secured" refers to the requirement that investors maintain enough cash in their brokerage account to finance the purchase of the underlying stock at the designated strike price if the buyer exercises the option. By selling cash-secured puts and collecting premiums up front, investors can make quick money. Should the buyer decide to execute the option before it expires, in return for the premium, the investor consents to buy the underlying shares at the strike price. When investors are optimistic about a company but would instead buy it at a discount or earn income while waiting for a suitable entry point, this approach may be alluring.

Selling cash-secured puts is mainly done to make money from the premiums received and buy stock below market value. Put options with a strike price less than the underlying company's current market value are known as out-of-the-money (OTM) puts. Investors sell these types of puts to profit from the options' time decay (theta) and the possibility that the stock price will still be higher at expiration. The investor keeps the premium received as profit without buying the underlying stock if the option expires worthless, which occurs when the stock price stays above the strike price. If the option is exercised and the stock price falls below the striking price, the investor will still need to purchase the shares at the strike price, but at a discount to the current market price.

Selling cash-secured options has several benefits, including the opportunity to produce money in neutral and bullish market conditions. The investor can keep the premium as profit if the stock price stays above the put options' strike price. The investor still gains from buying the shares at a discount to the going market price even if the price drops below the strike price. Furthermore, investors may purchase premium stocks at a cheaper cost through the sale of cash-secured puts than they would be able to pay if they were to buy them directly on the open market.

Selling cash-secured puts requires risk management because a significant decrease in the underlying stock price could result in considerable losses. Investors can use various methods, such as utilizing stop-loss orders, diversifying across various equities and strike prices, and choosing conservative strike prices to reduce this risk. Selling put options with strike prices considerably below the underlying company's current market price is setting cautious strike prices. This lowers the possibility that the option will be exercised, and the shares will be acquired at a disadvantageous price. Diversification among a number of stocks and strike prices aids in risk distribution and lessens susceptibility to fluctuations in a single stock. By automatically terminating put option positions if the underlying stock price drops below a predefined threshold, stop-loss orders can be utilized to reduce possible losses.

Selling cash-secured puts has some drawbacks that investors should be aware of, such as the requirement to pay the striking price for the underlying shares in the case that the trade is carried out. Investors should also be ready to retain the underlying stock for an extended period of time if needed, since selling cash- secured puts could result in equity ownership in the event that the option is executed. However, selling cash- secured puts can be a profitable tactic to take into consideration for investors looking to increase portfolio returns, create income, or purchase shares at a discount. To sum up, selling cash-secured puts is a smart way for investors to trade options strategically and maybe make money while buying stock at a discount to the going rate. Investors can profit from time decay and possible stock price gain in addition to collecting premiums up front by selling put options on companies they are willing to own. To reduce possible losses, investors must, however, be aware of the benefits and hazards of this strategy and have strong risk management procedures in place. Selling cash-secured puts can be a useful technique for investors looking to take advantage of market opportunities and increase their return on investment with careful planning, execution, and risk management.

Portfolio protection strategies

Investors who want to protect their investments and lessen the effects of market downturns, volatility increases, and unanticipated occurrences on their portfolios must implement portfolio protection methods. These tactics seek to lower downside risk, protect capital, and offer investors some degree of protection from unfavorable market swings. Investors can attain these goals through a variety of portfolio preservation techniques.

Diversification is a popular approach for protecting a portfolio. Spreading investments across several industries, geographies, and asset classes helps minimize exposure to any one investment or market niche. Investors can lessen the chance of suffering significant losses as a result of unfavorable events in a particular market or asset class by diversifying their holdings. An investor's investment portfolio can become more stable and robust with diversification, which can also improve risk-adjusted returns and smooth out portfolio returns over time.

The application of hedging procedures is another method of portfolio protection. Hedging reduces the risk of unfavorable price fluctuations in the underlying portfolio by holding offset positions in comparable assets or derivatives. An investor can, for instance, use put options on specific equities or stock index futures contracts to hedge their equity holdings. Put options allow investors to hedge against possible losses from drops in asset values by granting them the right to sell assets at a predefined price (the strike price) within a given time frame. Investors can reduce their exposure to downside risk and profit from potential upside profits by hedging their investments.

Investors can also use dynamic asset allocation techniques to safeguard their portfolios against shifting market conditions. In order to seize opportunities and lower risks, dynamic asset allocation modifies portfolio allocations in response to market outlook, economic data, and risk tolerance. For instance, during times of increased market volatility or uncertainty, investors should allocate more of their portfolio to defensive investments such as cash, bonds, or gold. On the other hand, at times of economic expansion or market confidence, they can raise their allocations to stocks or other risky assets. Investors can lessen the negative effects of volatile markets on their portfolios and respond to shifting market conditions by constantly modifying their asset allocations.

In addition, stop-loss orders and further risk-management techniques can also help shield portfolios from significant losses. With stop-loss orders, investors can limit possible losses by defining predefined price points at which they will sell their assets. For instance, investors can set up exchange-traded funds (ETFs) or individual stocks with stop-loss orders, which will cause the investments to be automatically sold if prices drop below a predetermined level. In the case of unfavorable market movements, stop-loss orders can help investors maintain discipline and restrict losses, giving them a measure of downside protection and peace of mind.

Investors might also wish to consider including alternative assets in their portfolios as a way to lower risk and boost profits. Alternative assets, which have low correlations with traditional asset classes like stocks and bonds, are essential to include in a broad portfolio. Examples of these assets include commodities, real estate, private equity, and hedge funds. In addition to offering additional sources of return and risk diversification, alternative investments can lower total portfolio volatility and improve risk-adjusted returns for investors. Investors can lessen the negative effects of market downturns on their overall investment performance and fortify their portfolio protection methods by adding alternative investments.

To sum up, investors who want to secure their money and lessen the effects of market volatility and unfavorable occurrences on their portfolios must implement portfolio protection techniques. Investors can safeguard their portfolios from significant losses and maintain wealth in fluctuating market situations by utilizing several important instruments such as diversification, hedging, dynamic asset allocation, risk management approaches, and alternative investments. Through the integration of these portfolio protection measures into their investment methodology, investors can augment their risk-adjusted returns, attain heightened stability, and adeptly manage the fluctuations of the financial markets.

Hedging individual positions versus overall portfolio

Investors use two risk management strategies to minimize possible losses and safeguard against unfavorable market movements: hedging individual positions and the entire portfolio. Various approaches have distinct functions and present varying advantages and disadvantages, contingent on the investor's goals, level of risk tolerance, and market conditions. Taking opposing positions in correlated assets or derivatives to counter the risk associated with particular holdings is known as hedging individual positions. Investors frequently employ this technique to secure individual position profits while hedging against short-term volatility and being exposed to overall market trends. For instance, by buying put options or selling call options on the same asset, an investor with a concentrated position in a single stock can protect themselves against downside risk. Investors can customize their risk management techniques to each investment in their portfolio, considering its distinct features and risk profile, by hedging individual positions.

Conversely, hedging the entire portfolio entails systemic actions to lower the investment portfolio's overall aggregate risk exposure. This strategy emphasizes asset allocation, diversification, and using tools for portfolio-level hedging to guard against market-wide downturns and systemic risks. Allocating assets among several asset classes, such as stocks, bonds, and alternative investments, is one way to distribute risk and lower correlation in portfolio-level hedging methods. Exchange-traded funds (ETFs), index options, and futures contracts are tools investors can use to protect themselves against general market fluctuations or declines in particular market segments. Regardless of how well individual positions within the portfolio perform, investors can safeguard themselves against systemic risks and market downturns by hedging the entire portfolio.

Hedging a portfolio as a whole and individual positions have benefits and drawbacks for investors. By providing focused risk management for specific holdings, hedging individual positions enables investors to guard against unfavorable price movements or short-term volatility in particular equities or assets. This strategy does, however, come with transaction costs related to carrying out hedging methods and the need for active position management and monitoring. Furthermore, if there is an imperfect correlation between the hedging instruments and the underlying assets, hedging individual holdings may restrict possible gains.

On the other hand, hedging the entire investment portfolio offers more comprehensive risk mitigation, making it less susceptible to market-wide downturns and systemic hazards. This strategy benefits investors who want to hedge against macroeconomic risks like interest rate fluctuations, world economic recessions, or geopolitical catastrophes. It is also helpful for investors with diversified portfolios. Nevertheless, because hedging instruments can hinder the entire portfolio's performance, portfolio-level hedging may reduce possible gains in bull markets or other times of solid market performance.

The decision to hedge a portfolio as a whole or individual positions is influenced by several variables, such as the investor's time horizon, risk tolerance, investing objectives, and market forecast. Investors may occasionally combine the two approaches to attain a well-rounded approach to risk management. For instance, investors can hedge their whole portfolio to reduce systemic risk and market-wide downturns while protecting individual positions from short-term volatility. Investors can customize their approach to risk management to meet their unique investing objectives and market conditions by combining various tactics.

In summary, investors can benefit from flexibility and protection against unfavorable market movements by implementing both individual position and portfolio hedging, which are complementary risk management techniques. Although single assets can be targeted for risk mitigation through individual position hedging, hedging the entire portfolio gives broader protection against market-wide downturns and systemic hazards.

Investors can create a complete risk management plan that fits their investing goals, risk tolerance, and market forecast by knowing the benefits and drawbacks of each technique. Hedging individual positions and the entire portfolio can help investors manage the volatility of the financial markets and achieve long-term investment success if they are correctly analyzed, put into practice, and monitored.

CHAPTER III

Managing Your Options Trades

Defining risk and managing it in an options context

In the world of options trading, capital preservation and success depend heavily on one's ability to recognize and manage risk. Risk is the potential for experiencing a loss or unfavorable consequences due to changes in the market, volatility, or other circumstances. Risk can take many different forms in the context of options, such as liquidity, time decay, volatility, and direction risks. The profitability of options contracts depends on the direction and size of price moves in the underlying asset, referred to as "directional risk." Changes in implied volatility give rise to volatility risk, which impacts the worth of options contracts and the possibility of profit or loss. Theta risk, sometimes called time decay risk, is the possibility that an option's value will decrease over time as expiration draws near, especially for options with longer expiration dates. Finally, because of narrow bid-ask spreads or insufficient market depth, liquidity risk concerns the ability to enter or exit options positions at desired prices.

In the context of options, managing risk entails the use of a range of strategies and techniques to reduce possible losses and safeguard money. Spreading risk across several options positions, underlying assets, or methods is one popular strategy called diversification. Diversification can improve portfolio resilience in unfavorable market moves and assist in lower exposure to risks associated with individual stocks or sectors. Position sizing is another technique for managing risk; it entails figuring out how much money to put into each option trade according to trading goals, portfolio size, and risk tolerance. Investors can reduce the possibility of catastrophic losses and limit the influence of individual transactions on the performance of their entire portfolio by managing position sizes about account size and risk tolerance.

Furthermore, options traders employ hedging as an essential risk management strategy to mitigate directional risk and guard against unfavorable market moves. Hedging strategies include buying protective puts (put options purchased to protect long stock positions), selling covered calls (put options sold against long stock positions to generate income), and using sophisticated spread strategies (collars, butterflies, etc.) to limit downside risk while preserving upside potential. These hedging techniques expose investors to possible gains while assisting in reducing losses in the event of unfavorable market changes.

Greeks are mathematical measures of many risk factors related to options contracts. Understanding and assessing them is another aspect of risk management in options trading. The Greeks, which include delta, gamma, theta, Vega, and rho, each shed light on how variations in the underlying asset's price, volatility, time decay, interest rates, and dividend yields affect the pricing of options. Traders who assess the Greeks of their options holdings and make the appropriate adjustments to their positions and methods can maximize their risk-return profiles, hedge against specific risks, and capitalize on market opportunities.

Furthermore, adhering to preset trading rules and standards and practicing disciplined trade execution is essential to risk control in options trading. Effective risk management requires establishing precise entry and exit criteria, establishing stop-loss orders, and routinely monitoring positions. Additionally, one can lessen the impact of unfavorable market conditions and limit liquidity risk by maintaining adequate liquidity and diversification across options positions, underlying assets, and expiration dates.

In summary, defining risk and managing it within the framework of options trading is essential for effective options trading. Directional risk, volatility risk, time decay risk, and liquidity risk are just a few variables that makeup risk in options trading. Each of these aspects calls for a different approach to risk management. Options traders can reduce risk, safeguard capital, and increase the likelihood of long-term success in the volatile and complex world of options trading by diversifying their portfolios, managing position sizes, using hedging techniques, examining the Greeks, and following disciplined trade execution.

Tools and techniques for risk assessment

Risk assessment is an essential part of making decisions in several fields, such as project management, environmental planning, and finance. It entails locating, assessing, and analyzing risks and their possible influence on goals and results. Individuals and organizations use various tools and techniques to help them make educated decisions and implement risk management strategies when assessing risk. A frequently employed instrument is the risk matrix, which graphically depicts the probability and seriousness of hazards according to predetermined standards. Stakeholders can arrange resources and prioritize response efforts by charting hazards on a matrix. Scenario analysis is another helpful method for looking at hypothetical situations and evaluating how they might affect goals. Decision-makers can achieve effective risk mitigation methods and excellent preparation for uncertainty by considering various conditions and their respective probabilities.

Probabilistic risk assessment is another effective method for putting risk into numerical terms and doing quantitative analysis. Evaluating the likelihood of different outcomes and the repercussions that accompany them enables stakeholders to make defensible decisions supported by data-driven insights and probabilistic models. Multiple simulations are run to represent the possible outcomes of complicated systems or processes using Monte Carlo simulation, a technique frequently employed in probabilistic risk assessment. Decision-makers can discover viable mitigation methods and understand risk exposure and variability by simulating thousands of alternative scenarios and their likelihoods.

Sensitivity analysis is also helpful in determining essential risk factors and evaluating how they affect results. Decision-makers can decide which factors are the most significant contributors to risk and focus their response efforts on them by methodically changing input parameters and tracking how those changes affect output variables. Sensitivity analysis assists stakeholders in identifying possible sources of uncertainty and creating effective backup plans to deal with them. Another risk assessment methodology is failure mode and effects analysis (FMEA), which methodically examines likely failure scenarios, their root causes, and their implications for goals. Organizations can reduce the chance of unfavorable events by putting controls and preventive measures in place by analyzing failure modes and their effects.

In addition, using qualitative risk assessment methods, including expert opinion, brainstorming sessions, and risk workshops, is essential for recognizing and evaluating challenging hazards to measure or quantify. Expert judgment is speaking with subject matter experts to get their opinions and thoughts on possible hazards and their effects. Stakeholders are encouraged to be creative and imaginative in risk assessment through collaborative idea development and risk identification during brainstorming sessions. Key stakeholders come together for risk workshops, where they debate and rank risks, create strategies for mitigating risks, and ensure that risk management goals and priorities are in line.

To sum up, efficient risk assessment necessitates a blend of instruments and methods customized to the particular situation and goals of the decision-making procedure. Stakeholders can obtain critical insights into potential risks, likelihoods, and potential impact on objectives by utilizing tools like risk matrices, scenario analysis, probabilistic risk assessment, sensitivity analysis, failure mode and effects analysis, and qualitative risk assessment techniques. Through systematic risk analysis and the creation of solid risk management plans, people and organizations may effectively reduce risks, improve decision-making, and confidently accomplish their goals in the face of uncertainty.

Developing a trading plan: Entry, exit, and adjustment strategies

Creating a trading plan is a vital first step for traders looking to negotiate the complex and frequently unpredictable world of financial markets. A well-defined trading plan outlines straightforward entry, exit, and adjustment methods, offering a disciplined framework for carrying out trades and managing risk. While exit strategies decide when to close a position to maximize profits or minimize losses, entry strategies specify the requirements and circumstances for starting a transaction. Adjustment methods are often used to adjust or hedge current positions in reaction to shifting market conditions. By combining these components into a coherent trading plan, traders can increase overall trading performance, optimize risk management, and strengthen their decision-making process.

Particular standards and indicators of profitable trading chances determine entry methods. Technical indicators like trendlines, moving averages, and chart patterns may be among these criteria, as well as fundamental elements like news stories, economic data releases, and earnings reports. Traders use these signals to pinpoint entry locations where they believe there is the best chance of success. A trend-following trader might, for instance, open a long position when the asset's price breaks above a crucial resistance level, indicating that the uptrend may continue. On the other hand, a contrarian trader who expects a reversal in the dominant trend can initiate a short position when the price hits an overbought condition. Entry signals should be objective, well-defined, and aligned with the trader's overall trading plan and risk tolerance, regardless of the technique used.

Since exit strategies dictate when to liquidate a position to reduce losses or achieve profits, they are equally significant. Setting profit targets, employing trailing stops, and putting predefined risk-reward ratios into practice are a few methods for determining exit points. The predefined price points at which traders plan to take profits and exit their positions are profit targets. Technical analysis, using prior support or resistance levels, Fibonacci retracement levels, or profit-taking zones found through trend analysis, is frequently the basis for these goals.

Dynamic stop-loss orders, known as "trailing stops," automatically modify as the asset's price rises to the trader's advantage. Trailing stops allow traders to lock in winnings while allowing the transaction to continue evolving. Furthermore, traders can employ predefined risk-reward ratios—like a 2:1 or 3:1—to ensure that possible gains on each trade exceed possible losses. Adjustment techniques are used to adjust or hedge current positions in reaction to shifting market conditions. These tactics support traders in efficiently managing risk and adapting to changing market conditions. Standard adjustment techniques include using hedging tactics, rolling options contracts, and adjusting into or out of positions. Scaling into or out of positions refers to gradually changing a position's size as the trade progresses. As a result, traders can minimize their exposure to possible losses while managing risk and taking advantage of favorable market moves. Rolling options contracts entail closing out current holdings and opening new ones simultaneously but with different expiration dates or strike prices. With the help of this method, traders can modify their exposure to variations in time decay, volatility, and other elements that impact the cost of options. To lower a portfolio's overall risk, hedging methods entail having opposing positions in correlated assets or derivatives. For instance, a trader can use put futures or options agreements pertaining to the same underlying asset to hedge a long stock position. In summary, traders hoping to succeed in the financial markets over the long run must create a trading plan that includes precise entry, exit, and adjustment techniques. While exit strategies decide when to shut out positions to maximize profits or minimize losses, entry strategies specify the requirements and circumstances for starting trades. In reaction to shifting market conditions, traders might adjust or hedge their current positions using adjustment techniques. By combining these components into a coherent trading plan, traders can increase overall trading performance, optimize risk management, and strengthen their decision-making process. It is imperative for traders to consistently assess and improve their trading strategies in light of changing market conditions, individual experiences, and feedback from their trading outcomes. Traders can successfully manage the complexity of financial markets and accomplish their trading objectives with discipline, patience, and a well-defined trading plan.

Trade execution: Timing, order types, and execution platforms

A critical factor in the effectiveness of trading methods in all financial markets is trade execution. To maximize prices and reduce transaction costs, entails the prompt and effective fulfilment of buy and sell orders. The proper execution platforms, time, and order types must all be carefully considered for successful trade execution. Because of the quick changes in the market that can affect asset prices and liquidity, timing is essential when executing trades. To choose the best moment to execute a deal, traders must evaluate market variables such as price movements, volatility, and liquidity levels. Technical indicators, market news, and economic data releases can all be analyzed by traders to help them pinpoint entry and exit points and execute their trades precisely so they can profit from favorable price changes.

Another essential component of trade execution is order types, which give traders directions on how they want their orders to be carried out in the market. Examples of common order types are market, limit, stop, and market-on-close orders. Market orders are executed instantly at the going rate, giving traders execution confidence but sometimes exposing them to unfavorable price slippage in quickly moving markets. Limit orders provide traders control over execution prices by allowing them to set a maximum price to purchase or a minimum price to sell. However, there is no certainty that an order will be executed if the market conditions do not fit the defined requirements. Stop orders are activated when the market price hits a predetermined level, enabling traders to minimize possible losses or enter trades at breakout opportunities. Market-on-close orders would allow traders to take part in price fluctuations at the end of the trading day. They are executed at the closing price of the trading session.

Because an execution platform gives you access to markets, liquidity, and order routing capabilities, choosing the correct one is essential for effective trade execution. The functionality, features, and price of execution platforms range from conventional brokerage platforms to sophisticated computerized trading systems and algorithmic trading platforms. When choosing an execution platform, traders must consider aspects including execution speed, dependability, cost structure, order routing choices, and market data accessibility. A platform that fits a trader's style and goals can also consider other elements like customer service, educational materials, and integration with different trading tools.

Technology has also changed the way that trades are executed, making it possible to use automated, algorithmic, and high-speed trading tactics. Algorithmic trading algorithms, often known as algos, are computer programs that automatically carry out trades according to pre-established standards like timing, volume, and price. These algorithms are able to detect trading opportunities and maximize execution outcomes by using statistical models and market data to execute transactions with millisecond precision. deals can be executed more quickly and effectively by using automated trading platforms, which enable traders to carry out deals automatically according to pre-established rules and criteria. This eliminates the need for human interaction.

In conclusion, timing, order types, and execution platforms must all be carefully considered for a good trade execution. In addition to choosing execution platforms that offer access to markets, liquidity, and order routing capabilities, traders also need to evaluate the state of the market. Trades can be executed quickly, precisely, and efficiently by using technology, such as automated trading platforms and algorithmic trading algorithms. This improves trading performance by optimizing execution results. In the dynamic and quick-paced world of financial markets, traders may successfully negotiate the intricacies of trade execution and accomplish their trading goals with the right preparation, analysis, and execution.

Monitoring open positions

In the financial markets, keeping an eye on open positions is essential to efficient portfolio management and risk reduction. Open positions are active trades that have been started but have yet to be finished. It is crucial to constantly monitor them to evaluate performance, control risk, and make wise decisions. Frequent monitoring enables traders and investors to assess market circumstances, keep tabs on the status of their open positions, and modify their methods as necessary to optimize profits and avoid losses. Traders can recognize new possibilities and dangers, profit from positive market movements, and lessen the likelihood of unfavorable outcomes by being alert and proactive in monitoring open positions.

Evaluating open jobs for initial goals and expectations is crucial to keeping an eye on them. Every open position needs to have its performance reviewed regularly by traders. They should compare goal price levels, initial entry points, and other pertinent metrics with the actual market prices and profit and loss levels. This study aids traders in evaluating the success of their trading plans, pinpointing areas in need of development, and making well-informed choices on the maintenance, modification, or closure of open positions. Furthermore, keeping an eye on open positions enables traders to spot possible red flags, like declining performance or unfavorable market developments, that can necessitate quick action to limit losses or preserve gains.

Monitoring available employment also requires careful consideration of risk management. The risk exposure of each open position and the portfolio as a whole, considering variables like position size, leverage, correlation, and market volatility, must be evaluated by traders. By surveilling risk parameters like value at risk (VaR), maximum drawdown, and portfolio beta, traders can detect possible weaknesses and execute suitable risk mitigation strategies, including modifying position sizes, hedging, or broadening their asset allocation. In market volatility and uncertainty, traders can maintain reasonable risk levels, safeguard money, and maintain long-term portfolio viability by routinely monitoring risk measurements.

By watching open positions, traders can also keep track of news stories and market movements that could affect their positions. Traders must remain current on economic indicators, corporate earnings releases, geopolitical shifts, and other events that may impact asset values and overall market sentiment. Traders can benefit from new possibilities and reduce risks by anticipating possible market developments, adjusting their positions accordingly, and staying educated and proactive.

Furthermore, by keeping an eye on open positions, traders can respond quickly to unforeseen circumstances or market shocks by modifying their methods or putting risk management procedures into place to reduce losses and save cash. Technology is essential for monitoring open positions since it gives traders access to trading platforms, analytics tools, and real-time market data. With features like position tracking, profit and loss analysis, configurable dashboards, and risk management tools, advanced trading platforms and software enable traders to effectively and efficiently monitor their open positions.

Furthermore, traders may manage their portfolios and keep an eye on their positions while on the road with the help of mobile trading apps, which guarantee prompt and well-informed decision-making under dynamic market conditions. In today's fast-paced financial markets, traders may stay competitive by using technology to gather actionable insights, automate the monitoring process, and keep a competitive advantage.

It's critical to monitor available openings in order to profitable trading and portfolio management. By consistently evaluating open positions' performance, risk, and market trends, traders can enhance their trading tactics, make well-informed decisions, and minimize possible losses. Vigilance, proactive risk management, and the utilization of technology to obtain real-time market data and analytics are all necessary for effective monitoring. Traders may confidently manage the intricacies of financial markets, seize opportunities, and accomplish their trading goals by remaining knowledgeable, disciplined, and adaptable.

It is not only a routine chore for traders and investors to keep an eye on open positions but also a strategic necessity as they navigate the constantly shifting and dynamic financial markets. Open positions are examples of active transactions that show traders' beliefs, plans, and expectations. Traders can evaluate these positions' performance, control risk, and make well-informed decisions to maximize profits and safeguard money by carefully monitoring them.

Evaluating open positions about initial goals and expectations is fundamental to monitoring. Key performance indicators, including market prices, profit and loss thresholds, and position size, must be routinely reviewed by traders and compared to entry points and target price ranges. With the help of this continuous analysis, traders may evaluate how well their trading techniques are working, pinpoint areas for development, and promptly modify their positions when the market conditions change.

Another crucial component of keeping an eye on available openings is risk management. Considering variables including position size, leverage, correlation, and market volatility, traders must evaluate the risk exposure of each position and the portfolio as a whole. By surveilling risk parameters like value at risk (VaR), maximum drawdown, and portfolio beta, traders can detect possible weaknesses and execute suitable risk mitigation strategies, including modifying position sizes, hedging, or broadening their asset allocation.

Furthermore, keeping up with news and market changes is crucial to efficiently tracking available positions. Traders need to stay current on various factors that could affect asset prices and market sentiment, such as company earnings releases, geopolitical happenings, and economic indicators. By being proactive and sensitive to market news and occurrences, traders can predict anticipated market changes, modify their positions, accordingly, take advantage of emerging opportunities, and reduce risks. Technology is essential for monitoring open positions since it gives traders access to trading platforms, analytics tools, and real-time market data. With features like position tracking, profit and loss analysis, configurable dashboards, and risk management tools, advanced trading platforms and software let traders keep an efficient eye on their open positions. Furthermore, traders may manage their portfolios and keep an eye on their positions while on the road with the help of mobile trading apps, which guarantee prompt and well-informed decision-making under dynamic market conditions.

To summarize, keeping an eye on open positions is essential to profitable trading and portfolio management. By consistently evaluating open positions' performance, risk, and market trends, traders can enhance their trading tactics, make well-informed decisions, and minimize possible losses. Vigilance, proactive risk management, and the utilization of technology to obtain real-time market data and analytics are all necessary for effective monitoring. Traders may confidently manage the intricacies of financial markets, seize opportunities, and accomplish their trading goals by remaining knowledgeable, disciplined, and adaptable.

Adjusting trades: When, why, and how

A key component of effective trading is trade adjustment, which enables traders to control risk, adjust to shifting market conditions, and optimize trading techniques for better results. Effective decision-making techniques, a solid grasp of risk management concepts, and a full awareness of market dynamics are necessary to determine when, why, and how to change deals. When unexpected occurrences affect the success of their positions or when their initial assumptions or expectations no longer match the market's state, traders adjust their trades. Changes in market patterns, volatility, economic data, or geopolitical events that impact asset prices and emotions in the market could cause this. Through vigilantly observing open positions and staying up to date with market trends, traders can detect any necessary adjustments to safeguard profits, curtail losses, or seize emerging chances.

The motivations for trade adjustments differ based on the trader's goals and unique situation. Readjusting deals is frequently done to manage risk successfully. Traders can modify their trades to lessen their exposure to unfavorable market moves, hedge against possible losses, or spread their risk across various assets or asset classes. To reduce potential losses, a trader might, for instance, change the size of their position, alter their entry or exit points, or use hedging techniques if a transaction begins to move against their expectations. Traders may also modify their deals to exploit profitable market trends or changes. Traders can maximize profits and capitalize on possible price changes by adjusting their holdings in response to emerging trends or market inefficiencies.

Essential considerations include market liquidity, volatility levels, and the trader's risk tolerance when determining whether to make trade modifications. Traders need to balance taking quick action to seize opportunities with waiting patiently to avoid making snap decisions in response to transient market swings. Risk-reward profiles must be evaluated, prospective outcomes must be carefully considered, and predetermined trading rules and guidelines must be followed to make effective trade changes. In addition, traders need to be objective and disciplined while making decisions, avoiding emotional biases and adhering to their trading plans even in the face of difficulty or ambiguity.

Traders have a variety of instruments and tactics at their disposal for adjusting deals. Examples of common adjustment tactics are scaling into or out of positions, rolling options contracts, changing strike prices or expiration dates, and putting hedging strategies into practice. Gradually expanding or decreasing position sizes in response to performance indicators and market conditions is known as "scaling into or out of" a position. By simultaneously closing out current positions and creating new ones with alternative strike prices or expiration dates, traders can modify their exposure to shifts in the market dynamics. This process is known as rolling options contracts. In erratic or unpredictable market conditions, hedging techniques like purchasing defensive puts or selling covered calls can assist traders in reducing risk and safeguarding earnings.

Furthermore, traders can think about modifying their trading plans or portfolio allocations in response to changing macroeconomic conditions or market patterns. For instance, a trader may adjust the allocations in their portfolio to take advantage of new possibilities or reduce risks if they notice a change in interest rates or a movement in market sentiment. Similarly, traders may tweak their approach by fine-tuning their entry and exit criteria, altering risk management guidelines, or diversifying across several trading methods or asset classes if their trading strategy no longer generates projected returns.

Making trade adjustments enables traders to manage risk efficiently, respond to shifting market conditions, and optimize trading techniques for better results. It is a crucial skill for successful trading. Knowing when, why, and how to alter transactions requires rigorous analysis, disciplined decision-making, and a deep comprehension of market dynamics and risk management concepts. By diligently monitoring open positions, staying up to date on market movements, and utilizing suitable adjustment strategies, traders can confidently manage the intricacies of financial markets and accomplish their trading goals. In the trading industry, adjusting transactions is both a talent and an art. It requires strategic thought, flexibility, and a clear sense of direction, like navigating a ship through constantly shifting waters. Traders who are skilled at trade adjustments can smoothly ride the market's ups and downs, maximizing their positions to take advantage of opportunities and reduce risks.

The fundamental component of trade modifications is the capacity to discern whether a deal requires tweaking. This realization frequently results from unforeseen circumstances that affect a position's performance or from a mismatch between initial expectations and the state of the market. Skilled traders closely monitor their open positions, prepared to make necessary modifications to safeguard profits or curtail losses in response to events, including changes in market patterns, elevated volatility, or unanticipated geopolitical developments.

The rationales behind trade adjustments are as diverse as the traders, representing their distinct situations, goals, and risk tolerance. Risk management serves as a primary motivator for trade adjustments. Traders adopt strategies, including position resizing, changing entry or exit points, or using hedging techniques to protect against potential losses, to change their positions and lessen their exposure to unfavorable market moves. Traders may handle tumultuous market situations more resilient and confident when actively managing risk. When it comes to trading adjustments, timing is everything. One must strike a careful balance between taking advantage of chances and being patient.

Prosperous traders know how important it is to take advantage of new trends or inefficiencies quickly. Still, they know when to use discipline to avoid making snap decisions based on transient changes. They retain discipline and impartiality even in the face of uncertainty by carefully analyzing possible outcomes, weighing risk-reward profiles, and abiding by predetermined trading rules and standards.

Traders can change transactions using various tools and methods available for execution. Traders can gradually modify their exposure in response to changing market conditions and performance measures by scaling into or out of positions. Rolling options contracts allow traders to respond to shifts in the market dynamics by modifying the strike price or the expiration date. At the same time, hedging techniques like covered calls and protective puts offer extra security in volatile markets.

Furthermore, astute traders may modify their overall trading methods or portfolio allocations if market trends or macroeconomic conditions change. They might reallocate funds to take advantage of newly created opportunities or diversify their holdings across several asset classes to reduce risk. Being flexible is essential for traders since they need to constantly review and improve their strategies to stay ahead of the curve in the fast-paced, always-changing financial markets of today.

Essentially, modifying deals involves carefully balancing analysis, intuition, and execution, making it both an art and a science. It calls on traders to be proactive, flexible, and quick to change course due to unanticipated developments or shifting market conditions. By being proficient in the art of trade adjustments, traders can become more adept at navigating the intricacies of financial markets and achieving their trading goals with assurance and accuracy.

CHAPTER IV

The Options Trader's Toolbox

Overview of trading platforms and tools

Trading platforms and tools, which give traders access to real-time market data, order execution capabilities, and analytical tools to enable well-informed decision-making, are essential for efficient and successful trading in financial markets. These tools and platforms are available in a variety of formats, from sophisticated electronic trading systems and algorithmic trading platforms to conventional brokerage platforms. The user interface of trading platforms, which enables traders to examine market data, make orders, and track their positions in real-time, is one of its main characteristics. With configurable dashboards, charting tools, and news feeds, traders can quickly evaluate market trends, spot trading opportunities and place trades thanks to intuitive interfaces.

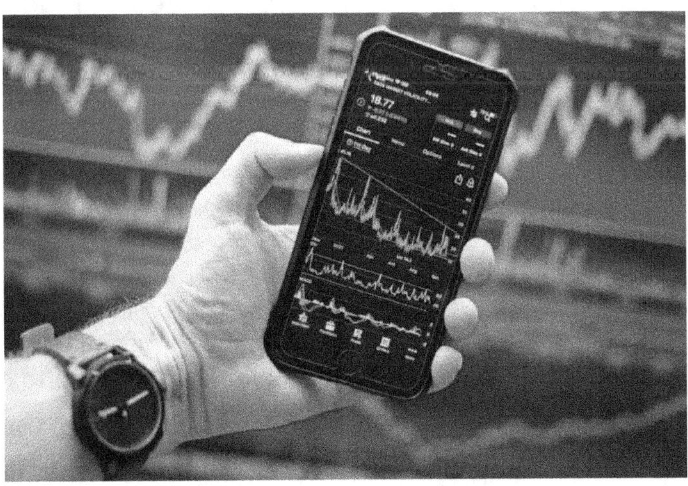

Another crucial element of trading platforms is market data, which gives traders access to volume, market depth, and historical and current pricing information. By examining market data, traders can discern patterns, trends, and correlations that empower them to make well-informed trading choices and effectively leverage market opportunities. Furthermore, traders can perform in-depth analysis of price movements, pinpoint support and resistance levels, and generate trading signals based on technical indicators like moving averages, RSI, MACD, and Bollinger Bands thanks to the sophisticated charting instruments and indicators of technical analysis that are frequently offered by trading platforms.

Trading platforms must include order execution capabilities to enable traders to place deals quickly and effectively. Trading systems allow traders to specify the price and conditions under which their orders should be executed. Examples of these order kinds are market orders, limit orders, stop orders, and conditional orders.

Furthermore, intelligent order routing (SOR) and direct market access (DMA) features are provided by modern trading platforms. These features allow traders to access numerous liquidity pools and execute trades at the best rates across many venues and exchanges.

Another crucial component of trading platforms is risk management tools, which allow users to control their exposure to risk and safeguard their wealth. Position sizing calculators, stop-loss orders, and margin monitoring tools are examples of risk management tools. These features assist traders in determining their degree of risk, establishing acceptable risk limits, and putting risk mitigation techniques into practice. Furthermore, risk analytics and performance tracking tools are frequently provided by trading platforms, enabling traders to track the performance metrics, drawdowns, and risk-adjusted returns of their portfolios over time.

Because they provide sophisticated automation and algorithmic trading capabilities, algorithmic trading platforms are becoming increasingly popular with institutional and retail traders. With the help of these platforms, traders may create, test, and implement trading algorithms that automatically execute deals by pre-established guidelines and standards. Various algorithms, such as trend-following, mean-reversion, arbitrage, and market-making methods, are available on algorithmic trading platforms, enabling traders to profit from various market circumstances and inefficiencies. Moreover, back testing features, optimization tools, and historical market data are frequently accessible through algorithmic trading platforms, allowing traders to enhance and optimize their algorithms for better results.

With the ability to monitor markets and manage positions while on the road, mobile trading apps have grown to be essential tools for traders. Many of the features and functionalities found in desktop trading platforms are also available in mobile trading apps, such as real-time market data, order execution capabilities, and charting tools. Furthermore, push alerts and notifications are frequently provided by mobile trading apps, enabling traders to remain updated on market movements and significant occasions that could affect their positions.

In order to provide traders with access to real-time market data, order execution capabilities, analytical tools, and risk management features, trading platforms and tools are vital elements of contemporary trading. Trading platforms are essential for traders that deal in stocks, forex, options, or cryptocurrencies since they allow them to manage their risk exposure, evaluate market trends, and execute transactions fast and effectively. Trading platforms are evolving along with technology, providing ever-more-advanced features and functionalities to cater to the needs of traders with varying degrees of experience and proficiency.

The use of trade management and analysis software has completely changed the way that trading is done today, giving traders access to a powerful toolkit that allows them to efficiently and accurately negotiate the intricacies of the financial markets. These software solutions, which range from complex trade management platforms to cutting-edge analytical tools, have grown to be essential tools for traders looking to obtain a competitive advantage and generate steady profits in the fast-paced trading environment of today.

The fundamental function of analytical software is its capacity to process and evaluate enormous amounts of market data in real-time, giving traders access to price movements, market trends, and trading opportunities. Trading professionals may see market data with unmatched clarity when equipped with sophisticated charting tools and technical indicators, allowing them to see patterns and trends that might be invisible to the unaided eye. Traders may make informed decisions and confidently execute winning trades with the tools provided by analytical software, which can be used for trend analysis, detecting support and resistance levels, or measuring momentum.

The analytical skills of traders are enhanced by trade management software, which offers powerful tools and capabilities for managing positions, tracking portfolio performance, and successfully implementing risk management measures. Trade management software, with its capabilities like position tracking, profit and loss analysis, and risk analytics, enables traders to determine how much risk they are taking, set suitable risk limits, and modify their positions in real time to maximize performance. Additionally, the trading process is streamlined through interaction with order execution systems, allowing traders to execute transactions quickly and easily in accordance with their analysis and trading plans.

Successful trading is based on risk management, and software solutions are essential for empowering traders to efficiently evaluate, track, and reduce risk. To assess risk levels and protect their cash, traders might use risk management software to place stop-loss orders, monitor margin requirements, and use position size calculators. Furthermore, risk management software provides advanced risk analytics and performance tracking capabilities, enabling traders to precisely and insightfully measure the risk-adjusted returns, drawdowns, and other critical performance parameters of their portfolio.

A new era of efficiency and automation has been brought about by the emergence of algorithmic trading software, which allows traders to use algorithms to execute transactions automatically based on predetermined rules and criteria. With a wide range of algorithms at their disposal, traders can profit from different market circumstances and inefficiencies with unmatched speed and accuracy. These algorithms include trend-following, mean-reversion, arbitrage, and market-making methods.

Algorithmic trading software also gives traders access to powerful back testing capabilities, historical market data, and optimization tools, enabling them to fine-tune and improve their algorithms for optimal efficiency and profit. Another vital tool in the trader's toolbox is trade journaling software, which gives traders a platform to track performance indicators, document and evaluate their trading activity, and pinpoint areas for development.

Trader insight, pattern recognition, and lesson learning can all be obtained by carefully recording transactions, including entry and exit points, trade justification, and performance results. A variety of analysis tools, performance statistics, and risk management metrics are also provided by trade journaling software, allowing traders to evaluate their performance impartially and decide on their trading tactics and practices.

In summary, trade management and analysis software is a fundamental component of contemporary trading, providing traders with the instruments and capacities necessary to prosper in the competitive and fast-moving financial markets of today. Traders rely on software solutions to automate trading methods, manage risk, analyze market trends, and journalize trades. This allows them to maximize performance, streamline processes, and accurately and efficiently accomplish their trading goals. Traders should anticipate even more sophistication and innovation in the tools and capabilities at their disposal as software solutions develop and technology advances, guaranteeing their place at the vanguard of trading excellence for years to come.

Software for analysis and trade management

Modern trading methods rely heavily on trade management and analysis software, which gives traders the tools and capabilities to effectively manage positions, evaluate market data, and execute transactions. These software programs are available in various formats, from stand-alone analytical instruments to all-inclusive trading platforms with integrated order execution, risk management, and analysis features. The capacity of analytical software to handle and evaluate massive amounts of market data in real-time, giving traders insights into price movements, market patterns, and trading opportunities, is one of its primary features. Traders can visualize market data, spot patterns, and create trading signals using sophisticated charting tools and technical indicators. Technical techniques such as momentum indicators, support and resistance levels, and trend analysis constitute the foundation of these instruments.

Another crucial element of contemporary trading is trade management software, which gives traders the instruments and capacities they need to control their positions, keep an eye on the performance of their portfolios, and put risk management plans into action. Trade management software enables traders to evaluate their risk exposure, establish suitable risk limits, and modify their holdings based on features like position tracking, profit and loss analysis, and risk analytics. Furthermore, order execution platforms and trade management software frequently interface to allow traders to rapidly and effectively execute transactions through their analysis and trading plans.

A crucial component of trade management is risk management, and software solutions give traders the instruments and capacities they need to properly evaluate, track, and reduce risk. With tools like stop-loss orders, margin monitoring, and position size calculators, risk management software enables traders to assess their risk tolerance, establish sensible risk thresholds, and implement risk mitigation plans. Furthermore, traders can track their portfolio's risk-adjusted returns, drawdowns, and other performance measures over time with the help of risk analytics and performance tracking tools frequently included in risk management software.

Traders are increasingly using algorithmic trading software since it provides sophisticated automation and algorithmic trading features. With these software programs, traders can create, test, and implement trading algorithms that automatically execute deals per pre-established guidelines and standards. Many algorithms, such as trend-following, mean-reversion, arbitrage, and market-making methods, are available through algorithmic trading software, enabling traders to profit from various market circumstances and inefficiencies. Moreover, back testing features, optimization tools, and historical market data are frequently accessible through algorithmic trading software, allowing traders to enhance and optimize their algorithms for better results.

Another helpful tool for traders is trade journaling software, which enables users to monitor performance indicators, document and evaluate their trading activity, and pinpoint areas for development. Traders can record their transactions using trade journaling software, including entry and exit points, trade justification, and performance results. A thorough trading record allows traders to see patterns, learn from past mistakes, and obtain meaningful insights into their trading routines.

Furthermore, trade journaling software frequently has functions like risk management measurements, trade analysis tools, and performance reports, which enable traders to evaluate their performance impartially and decide on trading tactics and procedures.

In summary, trade management and analysis software is crucial to contemporary trading. It gives traders the tools to effectively manage positions, evaluate market data, and execute trades. Traders rely on software tools to maximize their performance in today's fast-paced financial markets by streamlining their trading processes, controlling risk, automating trading methods, and evaluating market patterns. Software solutions constantly evolve due to technological advancements, providing traders with a broader range of features and functionalities to suit their demands, regardless of experience or degree of skill.

Analysis of successful trades and strategies

A vital skill for traders looking to boost their output, hone their methods, and secure steady profit in the financial markets is the analysis of profitable deals and strategies. Trades and strategies that are successful can control risk well, produce good returns over time, and adjust to shifting market conditions. In addition to gaining essential insights into the elements that led to successful trading, traders can also find patterns, trends, and best practices that can be repeated in subsequent trades by breaking down and evaluating successful bets.

Examining the decision-making process that precedes trade execution is crucial to good transaction analysis. The reasoning behind a trader's decisions must be evaluated, including studying market circumstances, identifying trading opportunities, and choosing suitable entry and exit locations. Through a critical examination of their reasoning and thought process, traders may pinpoint areas of strength and weakness in their decision-making and hone their analytical abilities to produce future trading decisions that are better informed and more successful.

In addition, assessing the performance of a deal entails determining how good the trading method used was. Traders need to evaluate if their approach fits in with their trading goals, risk tolerance level, and market prognosis. To ascertain their influence on trading results, they ought to scrutinize the particular features of the strategy, including entry and exit criteria, position sizing, and risk management guidelines. To evaluate the robustness and flexibility of the approach, traders should also consider how it performs in various market environments, periods, and asset classes.

Successful trading requires effective risk management, and evaluating the effectiveness of risk management techniques is a crucial part of successful transaction analysis. Traders must evaluate if their risk management policies sufficiently safeguarded capital and maintained profitability in challenging market circumstances. They should examine elements including position sizing, stop-loss placement, and portfolio diversification to ascertain their effect on risk-adjusted returns and overall portfolio performance. By identifying potential areas for improvement in risk management, traders can augment their capacity to safeguard capital and curtail losses in subsequent transactions.

Furthermore, studying the influence of psychology and emotions on trading decisions is necessary for analyzing profitable deals. Emotional reactions to profitable transactions, such as greed, arrogance, or FOMO (fear of missing out), must be evaluated by traders. Traders can create techniques to reduce emotional biases and uphold objectivity and discipline in decision-making by comprehending how emotions impact their trading behavior. To determine the elements that aided their capacity to carry out their trading strategy efficiently, traders need also examine their mentality and psychological condition during profitable deals.

Finding opportunities for trade technique and methodology optimization and improvement is another part of assessing profitable deals. To find inefficiencies, bottlenecks, and opportunities for improvement, traders should examine every step of their trading process, from market analysis to trade execution. They should consider adding new instruments, methods, or technological advancements to their trading toolbox to increase productivity, accuracy, and efficacy. To get more viewpoints and insights into their trading strategy, traders should also ask for comments from peers, mentors, or trading communities.

Analyzing profitable deals and techniques is crucial for traders looking to boost their efficiency and consistently turn a profit in the financial markets. By analyzing and assessing the elements that led to profitable trades, traders can learn a great deal about their decision-making processes, trading methods, risk tolerance, and mentality. In the fast-paced and cutthroat world of trading, traders can improve their abilities, adjust to shifting market conditions, and raise their prospects of long-term success by engaging in constant analysis, reflection, and optimization.

Examining profitable trades and methods is similar to reviewing the anatomy of a skilled trader, revealing the complex web of interwoven elements that produce positive results in the financial markets. Successful transactions are the result of careful research, wise decision-making, and systematic execution rather than being the result of chance or luck. Traders can gain priceless insights, improve their methods, and develop the experience required to regularly and accurately navigate the ups and downs of the market by closely examining the factors that lead to success.

A thorough analysis of the decision-making process that precedes trade execution is essential to understanding successful trade analysis. Traders need to examine the reasoning behind their trade choices, carefully reviewing their evaluation of the state of the market, finding trading opportunities, and choosing entry and exit locations. Through close examination of the underlying thinking and logic, traders can extract the key elements of effective decision-making, pinpointing areas of strength to strengthen and flaws to address. By engaging in this reflective process, traders can hone their analytical skills and make wise trading decisions based on a thorough comprehension of market dynamics and trends.

Moreover, assessing profitable transactions requires carefully evaluating the trading strategy's effectiveness. Traders must carefully consider if the plan they selected fits their trading goals, risk appetite, and market forecast well. To determine their effect on trading outcomes, they should carefully examine the strategy's unique parameters, including position sizing, risk management guidelines, and entry and exit criteria. To determine the strategy's robustness and flexibility, traders should also conduct a comprehensive stress test using a range of asset classes, timeframes, and market situations. Traders may create robust frameworks that withstand market volatility and time by distilling the essence of effective strategy design through introspection and review.

The foundation of effective trading is risk management, and evaluating successful trades requires a detailed evaluation of the risk management strategies used. Traders must carefully assess if risk management procedures protect their capital and maintain profits in challenging market circumstances. They must closely examine elements like position sizing, stop-loss placement, and portfolio diversification to understand how vital aspects affect risk-adjusted returns and portfolio performance overall. Traders can decrease the danger of catastrophic losses in future trades and strengthen their defenses against market volatility by identifying areas for optimization and enhancement in risk management.

Furthermore, examining profitable trades requires delving deeply into the complex interactions between psychology and emotions when trading decisions. Traders need to be honest about how they feel after making a profitable trade, looking deeply into emotions like greed, arrogance, or FOMO that can erode discipline and impair judgment. Traders can create techniques to reduce emotional biases and promote a resilient and calm mentality in the face of market changes by developing self-awareness and introspection. Traders should also analyze their mental states during profitable transactions, pinpointing the cognitive processes that enabled them to carry out their trading strategy efficiently. By engaging in this process of psychological reflection, traders can develop the mental toughness and emotional stability required to handle the psychological ups and downs of trading with poise and dignity.

Moreover, examining profitable transactions requires a constant search for optimization and improvement in trading strategies and tactics. Traders should closely examine every aspect of their trading process, from trade execution to market analysis, to find inefficiencies, bottlenecks, and opportunities for improvement. They ought to maintain an open mind regarding adding new instruments, methods, or technological advancements to their trading toolkit, viewing innovation as a driving force behind increased efficacy, precision, and efficiency.

Furthermore, it is advisable for traders to proactively solicit input from mentors, peers, or trading forums. They can obtain new perspectives on their trading methodology by utilizing the combined knowledge and varied viewpoints. Using an unwavering dedication to perpetual enhancement and novelty, traders can foster a competitive advantage and adjust to the constantly changing terrain of financial markets.

In summary, traders who want to improve their performance and consistently make money in the financial markets must analyze profitable deals and tactics. By dissecting the components that support success, traders can solve the puzzles of successful decision-making, strategy development, risk management, and psychological toughness. In the fast- paced and cutthroat world of trading, traders may hone their craft, adjust to shifting market conditions, and set themselves up for long-term success by engaging in constant self-reflection, assessment, and optimization.

Lessons from failed trades

Analyzing losing transactions is a crucial exercise for traders looking to boost their performance, hone their tactics, and learn from their mistakes in the financial markets. Trade failures, marked by losses or less-than- ideal results, can teach traders essential lessons about where their decision-making, risk-taking, trading, and psychological approaches are lacking. Traders can identify areas for development and create techniques to prevent repeating the same mistakes by analyzing unsuccessful transactions and figuring out what went wrong.

A crucial takeaway from unsuccessful transactions is the significance of organized risk control. Traders must evaluate if their risk management policies were followed correctly and if their capital was sufficiently safeguarded in volatile markets. Inadequate risk management, such as taking on excessive holdings, diversifying too little, or not using stop-loss orders, frequently leads to unsuccessful trades. Traders should assess their risk management methods, including portfolio diversification, position sizing, and stop-loss placement, to find areas for improvement and create plans for future trades that will reduce risk more successfully.

Failed trades also emphasize the significance of careful due diligence and market analysis. Traders must evaluate if they made their trade selections based on a solid technical, fundamental, and sentimental analysis of the market conditions. Missing or faulty market analysis can lead to traders entering positions based on erroneous assumptions or missing information, resulting in unsuccessful trades. To make more informed and precise trade judgments in the future, traders should assess their analysis process, including data sources, analytical tools, and decision-making criteria, to find any gaps or flaws and improve their analytical abilities.

Additionally, losing trade can teach you a lot about the psychology and emotional impact of trading. Traders must evaluate how much their psychological predispositions and feelings affect their trading and decision-making. Emotional reactions like greed, revenge trading, fear of missing out (FOMO), or overconfidence can result in failed deals because they cause traders to stray from their trading plan or disregard risk management guidelines. To detect triggers, traders should examine their psychological condition and emotional state during losing trades. They should then build ways to reduce emotional biases and preserve objectivity and discipline in their trading.

The significance of flexibility and adaptation in trading tactics is further highlighted by unsuccessful deals. It is vital for traders to assess if they were able to adjust their trading strategies in response to changing market conditions and whether they did so when required. Failure to notice changes in market patterns, volatility levels, or underlying fundamentals can result in failed transactions as traders continue to use no longer profitable techniques. To find areas for adaptation, traders should evaluate their methods and strategies. Then, they must devise strategies for reversing or altering their direction in reaction to changing market conditions.

Unsuccessful transactions further highlight a trader's need for ongoing education and development. Traders must adopt a growth mindset and view setbacks as chances for personal development and education rather than as unavoidable losses. Over time, traders can improve their abilities, methods, and strategies with insightful feedback from unsuccessful deals. Traders should implement a continuous improvement process, solicit input from peers, mentors, or trading forums, and apply the lessons they've learned from losing trades to their trading approach in order to become more resilient, adaptive, and successful over time. Being an influential trader in the financial markets requires analyzing losses on trades. By breaking down unsuccessful transactions and analyzing the causes that led to their failure, traders can acquire important insights into areas for development in their decision-making process, trading tactics, risk management techniques, and psychological mentality. Traders can improve their prospects of long-term success in competitive and dynamic markets by developing the resilience, discipline, and abilities necessary to overcome trading's hurdles through introspection, adaptation, and continual learning.

It is a good exercise for traders looking to get better at what they do and an essential step in learning the nuances of the financial markets. Even though they might be frustrating or disappointing, lost trades are great teaching moments that reveal a lot about a trader's decision-making process, strategy execution, approach to risk management, and psychological fortitude. Through a thorough analysis of unsuccessful transactions and comprehending the underlying reasons for their failings, traders can uncover critical insights that help them develop, improve, and eventually succeed in the complex world of trading.

The critical takeaway from examining unsuccessful transactions is the importance of practicing rigorous risk management. Traders must assess critically if they adequately protected their capital amid volatile market conditions and whether their risk management processes were implemented correctly. Risk management mistakes, like being overexposed to one position, having too little diversification, or not having stop-loss orders, are often the cause of unsuccessful trades. By going over their risk management tactics in detail— including position sizing, stop-loss placement, and portfolio diversification—traders may identify areas that require improvement and develop plans to strengthen their risk mitigation strategies going forward.

Failed transactions also serve as emotional reminders of how crucial it is to perform in-depth due diligence and market analysis. Traders need to carefully consider if they based their trade selections on solid technical, fundamental, and sentiment research of the market environment. Incomplete or inaccurate market analysis frequently leads to unsuccessful trades because it causes traders to take positions based on false assumptions or insufficient knowledge. Traders can pinpoint shortcomings and improve their analytical skills to make more precise and informed trade judgments in the future by reevaluating their analysis process, which includes the caliber of data sources, effectiveness of analytical tools, and strictness of decision-making criteria.

Furthermore, losing trades might shed light on how important psychology and emotions are to trading. It is imperative for traders to engage in introspection to determine whether their psychological biases and emotional state impacted their trading behavior and decision-making. Emotional reactions like greed, overconfidence, fear of missing out (FOMO), or revenge trading can seriously cloud judgment and sway traders from following their well thought out risk management or trading strategies. Traders can reduce emotional biases, promote discipline, and develop objectivity in their trading strategy by honestly assessing their psychological attitude and emotional triggers following unsuccessful trades.

Failed transactions also highlight how important it is for trading methods to be flexible and adaptive. Traders need to assess if their approaches to trading were flexible enough to adapt to changing market conditions and if they showed the ability to change course when necessary. Traders are frequently forced to stick with outdated or ineffective techniques after failing to recognize shifts in market patterns, volatility levels, or underlying fundamentals. By carefully analyzing their trading strategies and procedures, traders can pinpoint areas that lend themselves to adaptability and devise strategies to modify or reconsider their approach in light of changing market circumstances.

Failed trades also highlight the critical importance of ongoing learning and development in trading. Traders need to have a growth mentality and see defeats as necessary learning opportunities rather than as crippling catastrophes. Failed trades provide priceless input that can be used to strengthen tactics, improve techniques, and sharpen abilities over time. In order to become more resilient, adaptable, and ultimately successful traders in the fast-paced and cutthroat world of financial markets, traders can seek feedback from mentors, peers, or trading communities and incorporate the lessons learned from losing trades into their trading toolkit.

In conclusion, one of the most important aspects of learning to trade successfully in the financial markets is to analyze lost deals. Through an in-depth analysis of the underlying reasons behind unsuccessful trades and the richness of knowledge they contain, traders may pinpoint areas where their decision-making, trading, risk-taking, and psychological toughness could use some improvement. By means of self-reflection, flexibility, and a resolute dedication to lifelong learning, traders can develop the fortitude, self-control, and expertise necessary to effectively handle the complex obstacles of the trading profession and increase their chances of sustained success in the volatile and harsh world of financial markets.Top of Form

Resources for continuous learning and market updates

Within the ever-changing realm of financial markets, traders who want to improve their abilities, remain informed, and adjust to shifting market conditions must practice continuous learning and remain up to date with market changes. Thankfully, traders have access to many tools that offer insightful instructional materials, market research, and up-to-date information to aid in their learning and decision-making. These materials are available to traders with varying degrees of experience and skill and come in various formats, such as online courses, webinars, podcasts, newsletters, research papers, and social media channels.

Structured learning programs are available through online courses and instructional platforms, giving traders a thorough understanding of various trading and investing topics. These courses give traders a solid basis to expand upon by covering technical analysis, fundamental analysis, risk management, trading psychology, and strategy building. With the use of interactive materials, tests, assignments, and certifications, many online courses enable traders to study at their own pace and monitor their development as they move through the course material. Furthermore, online courses frequently offer access to knowledgeable instructors, trading simulations, and community forums. In these spaces, traders can communicate with mentors and peers to work through ideas, exchange insights, and explore issues.

Live events and webinars allow traders to pick the brains of analysts, market professionals, and seasoned traders in real time. The real-time offer traders insightful opinions and viewpoints from seasoned specialists on various subjects, such as market analysis, trading strategies, risk management tactics, and industry trends. Webinars allow traders to connect directly with speakers and obtain practical demos, case studies, and interactive Q&A sessions. This gives traders actionable insights into their trading processes. Furthermore, webinars give traders the chance to network with mentors, colleagues, and business executives, encouraging cooperation and knowledge exchange among traders.

Traders are increasingly using podcasts as a popular way to listen to educational content and get market updates while on the road. Podcasts include interviews with successful traders, market analysis, trading psychology, and discussions of current affairs and financial market trends, among many other topics. Experienced traders, analysts, and business experts frequently discuss their thoughts, tactics, and takeaways from their market experiences in podcasts. Podcasts are a great tool for lifelong learning and staying up to speed with market news and trends since they provide traders with an easy method to stay informed and involved with developments when traveling, working out, or doing other activities. Delivered straight to traders' inboxes, newsletters and research papers offer carefully selected material, market analysis, and practical insights. These magazines assist traders stay informed about significant events and trends influencing financial markets. They address a variety of topics, including market commentary, economic indicators, corporate earnings reports, and geopolitical happenings. Reputable brokerage houses, independent analysts, and financial institutions generate a plethora of research reports and newsletters that give traders access to superior research and analysis to help guide their trading decisions. Furthermore, newsletters are a great source for traders looking for ongoing education and market updates because they frequently contain trading ideas, educational information, and advice for enhancing trading success.

Social media sites like LinkedIn, Twitter, and trading forums give traders a place to interact with other traders, exchange ideas, and remain up to current on news and trends in the market in real time. Social media is a popular platform for traders and business professionals to exchange market commentary, analysis, trading ideas, and instructional information. This allows traders to gain important insights and viewpoints from a variety of sources. Furthermore, social media platforms facilitate collaboration and knowledge sharing among traders by giving them the chance to participate in discussions, pose questions, and gain knowledge from analysts, instructors, and seasoned traders.

Resources for ongoing education and market updates are essential for traders who want to improve their abilities, remain current on developments in the market, and adjust to shifting circumstances. Traders can access a multitude of instructional materials, market analysis, and up-to-date information via social media platforms, webinars, podcasts, online courses, and newsletters, among other resources, to aid in their learning and decision-making. Through efficient utilization of these tools, traders can raise their prospects of success in the modern, ruthless world and dynamic financial markets, stay ahead of the curve, and hone their trading methods. Not only are ongoing education and market awareness advised behaviors for traders, but they are also necessary routines that can spell the difference between success and failure in the volatile and rapidly evolving world of financial markets. Since information and technology are always at our fingertips, traders have an abundance of resources at their disposal to aid in their educational process and keep them up to date on opportunities, events, and market trends. Through efficient utilization of these resources, traders can improve their abilities, hone their trading tactics, and adjust to shifting market circumstances with assurance and dexterity.

Online courses and educational platforms, which offer structured learning programs aimed to give traders extensive information and abilities in all aspects of trading and investment, are among the most significant resources accessible to traders. These courses are designed for traders with varying degrees of experience and competence, covering a wide range of topics like as technical analysis, fundamental analysis, risk management, trading psychology, and strategy building. Online courses provide traders with the flexibility to keep track of their progress and learn at their own speed as they move through the curriculum thanks to interactive content, quizzes, assignments, and certificates. Additionally, access to knowledgeable instructors, trading simulators, and community forums are frequently offered by online courses, allowing traders to communicate with mentors and peers to work together on trading ideas, discuss topics, and share insights.

Another useful tool for traders is webinars and live events, which offer the chance to pick the brains of analysts, market experts, and seasoned traders in real time. These gatherings provide traders helpful insights and viewpoints from seasoned professionals on a variety of subjects, such as market analysis, trading strategies, risk management tactics, and industry trends.

Webinars give traders the chance to connect directly with speakers and obtain practical insights into their trading techniques through interactive Q&A sessions, case studies, and practical demonstrations. Furthermore, webinars give traders the chance to network with mentors, colleagues, and business executives, encouraging cooperation and knowledge exchange among traders.

A common way for traders to get market updates and educational content while on the go is through podcasts. Podcasts provide traders with an easy way to stay informed and involved with market developments while driving, working out, or doing other activities. Topics covered include market analysis, trading psychology, interviews with successful traders, and discussions on current events and trends in financial markets. Podcasts offer insightful viewpoints and perspectives that can guide traders' trading decisions and assist them in more skillfully navigating the complexities of financial markets. They feature seasoned traders, analysts, and industry professionals expressing their knowledge, tactics, and takeaways from their market experiences.

Delivered straight to traders' inboxes, newsletters and research papers offer traders carefully selected material, in-depth market analysis, and practical insights. Newsletters and research papers that cover subjects including economic indicators, company earnings reports, geopolitical developments, and market commentary assist traders in staying up to date on significant occurrences and patterns influencing the financial markets. These publications, which are produced by respectable brokerage houses, financial institutions, and independent analysts, provide traders with access to excellent research and analysis to help them make trading decisions.

Furthermore, newsletters are a great source for traders looking for ongoing education and market updates because they frequently contain trading ideas, educational information, and advice for enhancing trading success.

Social media sites like LinkedIn, Twitter, and trading forums give traders a place to interact with other traders, exchange ideas, and remain up to current on news and trends in the market in real time. Social media is a popular platform for traders and business professionals to exchange market commentary, analysis, trading ideas, and instructional information. This allows traders to gain important insights and viewpoints from a variety of sources. Social media platforms also facilitate collaboration and knowledge sharing among traders by giving them the chance to participate in discussions, pose questions, and gain knowledge from analysts, educators, and seasoned traders.

To sum up, tools for lifelong learning and market news are vital for traders who want to improve their abilities, remain current, and adjust to shifting market conditions. Traders can access a multitude of instructional materials, market analysis, and up-to-date information via social media platforms, webinars, podcasts, online courses, and newsletters, among other resources, to aid in their learning and decision-making. Through efficient utilization of these tools, traders can raise their prospects of success in the cutthroat world of today and dynamic financial markets, stay ahead of the curve, and hone their trading methods.

Building a network of traders and experts

A helpful tactic for traders looking to improve their abilities, obtain new perspectives, and increase their possibilities in the financial markets is establishing a network of traders and experts. A network of specialists and traders gives traders access to a wide range of viewpoints, experiences, and knowledge, enabling them to exchange ideas, work together on trading methods, and learn from others. Creating a network of traders and specialists has many advantages, such as providing access to insightful information, fostering collaborative opportunities, and providing peer and mentor support.

Access to insightful viewpoints and important insights is one of the main advantages of establishing a network of traders and specialists. The network's traders and experts contribute many skills and expertise, providing unique insights into market trends, trading tactics, risk control methods, and mentalities. Traders can increase the breadth of their market knowledge, question their preconceptions, and obtain fresh insights by interacting with peers and mentors inside the network. Furthermore, networking gives traders the chance to take lessons and insights from the triumphs and mistakes of others, which they can use in their trading methods.

Additionally, networking offers dealers chances for cooperation and partnership. By working together, traders and specialists can take advantage of one another's resources, skills, and strengths to accomplish shared goals and objectives. To access markets and opportunities unavailable to individual traders, traders work together on research projects, create trading methods, exchange trade ideas, and even pool resources. Cooperation within the network creates a supportive atmosphere where traders may grow, learn, and achieve together by fostering a sense of community and camaraderie among traders.

Creating a network of specialists and traders also gives traders access to peers and mentors who can help and encourage them. Trading can be a lonesome pursuit, and the journey has many obstacles, disappointments, and unknowns. Traders can obtain direction, counsel, and encouragement to handle the ups and downs of trading with confidence and resiliency by creating a network of encouraging peers and mentors. Within the network, mentors and peers can share victories, offer support during trying times, and hold traders accountable for maintaining discipline and goal focus.

Through networking, traders can also utilize mentorship and professional growth opportunities. Experts and seasoned traders in the network can act as mentors, providing direction, counsel, and support to novice traders aiming to advance their abilities and accomplish their trading goals. Through individualized guidance and criticism, mentoring helps traders pinpoint areas for growth, hone their trading techniques, and get past roadblocks. Furthermore, networking gives traders access to training courses, professional development opportunities, and instructional materials to increase their trading knowledge and proficiency.

A helpful tactic for traders looking to improve their abilities, obtain new perspectives, and increase their possibilities in the financial markets is creating a network of traders and experts. A network of specialists and traders gives traders access to insightful information, teamwork chances, peer and mentor assistance, professional development opportunities, and mentorship. Traders may learn from others, exchange ideas, work together on trading methods, and gain access to chances and resources that can help them thrive in today's competitive and dynamic trading environment by interacting with peers and mentors within the network. Developing a network of traders and specialists is more than just adding more people to your social circle; it's about uniting like-minded people passionate about trading and dedicated to helping each other succeed. Creating a network of traders and specialists has never been more straightforward or more accessible, thanks to technology's ability to facilitate real-time communication and collaboration in today's interconnected world. But it takes more than simply reaching out to people on social media or going to business gatherings; it takes a purposeful and calculated strategy to build a community of support and genuine relationships.

Access to insightful viewpoints and important insights is one of the main advantages of establishing a network of traders and specialists. A trader's grasp of the markets and trading methods can be expanded by utilizing the distinct experiences, skills, and expertise each trader brings. Traders can share ideas, best practices, and lessons from each other's successes and failures by conversing with peers and mentors in the network. Traders can challenge their preconceptions, obtain fresh insights, and improve their trading strategy by drawing on the network's collective knowledge to adjust to shifting market conditions.

Additionally, networking allows traders to work together and form partnerships, improving their trading skills and creating new prospects for expansion and profit. Traders can take advantage of one another's resources, skills, and talents by working with other traders and experts in the network to accomplish shared goals. Collaboration stimulates creativity, innovation, and synergy among participants in various activities, such as doing cooperative research, creating trading methods, or exchanging trade ideas. Traders can access markets and opportunities that may be out of their reach by combining their knowledge and resources, increasing their chances of success in the cutthroat trading world.

Creating a network of traders and specialists also fosters a positive atmosphere where traders can find responsibility, inspiration, and support to maintain concentration and discipline on their trading objectives. A solitary and somewhat isolating endeavor, trading frequently presents its practitioners with obstacles, disappointments, and uncertainty. Maintaining one's tenacity and morale throughout difficult times can be significantly aided by having a network of mentors and peers to draw on. Within the network, mentors and peers can provide direction, counsel, and emotional support, enabling traders to weather the highs and lows of trading with courage and fortitude.

Furthermore, networking gives traders access to professional development and mentoring opportunities, both critical for the ongoing advancement and development of trading. Experts and seasoned traders in the network can act as mentors, providing insightful advice, constructive criticism, and direction to novice traders looking to advance their expertise. Through individualized guidance and assistance, mentoring helps traders pinpoint areas for growth, get past challenges, and quicken their learning curve. Additionally, networking provides access to training courses, professional development opportunities, and instructional materials that can enhance traders' trading knowledge and proficiency.

To sum up, creating a network of traders and experts is a wise investment in one's trading profession that can pay off well in terms of knowledge, chances, assistance, and personal development. Traders can obtain essential insights, work together on trading methods, receive support and encouragement, and access mentorship and professional growth possibilities by actively interacting with peers and mentors inside the network. In the end, a robust network may act as a rock of support and resiliency for traders, allowing them to successfully negotiate the complexities of the financial markets with assurance, flexibility, and success.

CHAPTER V

Beyond the Basics

How economic, political, and global events affect options trading

Global, political, and economic events affect asset prices in financial markets, market sentiment, and volatility levels, which significantly affect options trading. These can include geopolitical developments like elections, trade talks, and geopolitical tensions, as well as macroeconomic indicators like interest rate decisions, inflation data, and GDP growth statistics. Global occurrences like pandemics, natural disasters, and economic downturns can significantly impact options trading. To predict how these occurrences might affect market circumstances, traders must closely watch and evaluate them. Then, they must modify their options trading techniques as necessary.

Market mood and volatility levels are two main ways economic, political, and international events impact options trading. The demand for riskier assets may rise in response to positive economic or political developments, which will raise investor confidence, option prices, and implied volatility levels. On the other hand, unfavorable economic information or tense geopolitical situations can sour investor mood and increase market ambiguity, which drives down option prices and raises volatility. By modifying their options trading tactics to seize profitable opportunities or protect against prospective losses, traders can profit from shifts in market mood and volatility.

Events that affect the price and volatility of the underlying asset, such as corporate earnings announcements, central bank meetings, and employment figures, can also affect options trading. For instance, a company's stock price and implied volatility levels may climb in response to better-than-expected earnings reports; this could raise the value of call options and present chances for traders to profit from bullish strategies like long calls or bull spreads. Similarly, a bad economic report or unfavorable news story may cause the price and volatility of the underlying asset to drop, giving traders a chance to profit from bearish strategies like long puts or bear spreads. Politics events can also significantly impact options trading, mainly if they cause volatility or uncertainty in the market. For instance, elections, referendums, or changes in the administration may result in changes to regulations, policy, or geopolitical conflicts that affect asset prices and market sentiment. In advance of these events, traders may modify their options trading methods by taking speculative positions to profit from expected market movements or by hedging their positions to guard against potential losses. Furthermore, political events like trade agreements, diplomatic disputes, or armed wars can cause uncertainty and volatility on the marketplace, enabling dealers to make money from options techniques meant to take advantage of variations in volatility.

Global occurrences like pandemics, natural catastrophes, or economic crises can also affect the options trading industry by generating changes in investor attitudes, upsetting supply networks, or disrupting economic activity. For instance, a broad outbreak of an infectious disease like COVID-19 might result in lockdowns, travel bans, and economic downturns that affect investor confidence, consumer purchasing, and company profits. In reaction to these developments, traders may modify their options trading methods by taking speculative positions to profit from expected market movements or by hedging their positions to guard against downside risk.

Global, political, and economic events significantly impact options trading; they affect asset values in financial markets, market sentiment, and volatility levels. To predict how these occurrences might affect market circumstances, traders must closely watch and evaluate them. Then, they must modify their options trading techniques as necessary. By remaining knowledgeable and proactive, traders may take advantage of profit- making opportunities, protect themselves from potential losses, and negotiate the intricacies of today's dynamic and interconnected global markets.

Financial market swings result from global, political, and economic events that also affect asset values, investor sentiment, and volatility levels. Options traders must comprehend the significant influence of these events to efficiently adjust their trading techniques and make well-informed judgments. These events cover a broad spectrum of variables, each with specific ramifications for options trading, from global crises and natural disasters to macroeconomic indicators and political developments. Events in the economy, politics, and the world significantly impact options trading, primarily through their influence on market mood and volatility levels. Good economic news, such as healthy corporate results or strong GDP growth, tends to bolster investor confidence and drive-up demand for riskier assets, which drives up option prices. This increase in demand frequently results in higher implied volatility levels as investors look to hedge against possible losses. On the other hand, unfavorable economic data or increased geopolitical tensions can erode investor confidence, leading to a flight to safety and a decrease in option prices as volatility rises. By modifying their options trading techniques, traders can take advantage of market mood and volatility changes to seize profitable chances or protect themselves from future losses.

Economic events influencing options trading activity include central bank meetings, job figures, and earnings announcements. For instance, the Federal Reserve's unexpected decision to raise interest rates may significantly affect asset prices and market volatility, allowing traders to profit from volatility-based trading methods like strangles and straddles. Similarly, directional techniques like long calls or puts can enable traders to profit from sudden price fluctuations in specific stocks following corporate earnings reports. A trader can position themselves to profit from market movements and volatility changes by keeping up to date on anticipated economic events and their possible effects on options trading.

Events in politics can also greatly influence options trading, mainly if they cause volatility or uncertainty in the market. Elections, referendums, and changes in the administration might result in regulatory modifications, policy changes, or geopolitical conflicts that affect asset prices and market sentiment. In advance of these events, traders may modify their options trading methods by taking speculative positions to profit from expected market movements or by hedging their positions to guard against potential losses. Furthermore, geopolitical events like trade agreements, diplomatic disputes, or armed wars can cause uncertainty and volatility on the marketplace, enabling dealers to make money from options techniques to take advantage of variations in volatility.

Global occurrences like pandemics, natural catastrophes, or economic crises can significantly impact the options trading industry by generating changes in investor attitudes, upsetting supply networks, or disrupting economic activity. For instance, the COVID-19 epidemic caused severe market turbulence and a flight to safety, with investors putting their money in government bonds and gold, two safe-haven investments. In reaction to these developments, traders may modify their options trading methods by taking speculative positions to profit from expected market movements or by hedging their positions to guard against downside risk. By closely monitoring worldwide events and their possible effects on financial markets, traders can position themselves to take advantage of new chances and maneuver through unstable market situations.

In summary, political, economic, and international events significantly influence market sentiment, volatility, and asset prices, which also serve as significant catalysts for options trading activity. To take advantage of profit-making possibilities, protect themselves from potential losses, and negotiate the intricacies of today's dynamic and interconnected global markets, traders need to be alert and proactive in monitoring these occurrences and modifying their options trading tactics accordingly. In the constantly shifting world of options trading, traders can position themselves for success by remaining knowledgeable, flexible, and disciplined.

Sector-specific options strategies

Customizing options trading techniques to take advantage of opportunities and reduce risks within particular economic sectors is known as sector-specific options strategy. Certain industries have particular traits, like market dynamics, volatility, and fundamental drivers, which might present different trading possibilities for options traders. Traders can enhance their trading performance and augment their prospects of success by comprehending the subtleties inherent in each sector and executing sector-specific methods for options.

In the technology industry, using covered calls is one options technique that is sector specific. Given its reputation for volatility and rapid growth, the technology sector is a desirable choice for covered call strategies. To make extra money, traders can purchase shares of technological companies with promising futures and then sell covered call options against their holdings. Traders can earn from the premium gained by selling covered calls, and if the stock price rises, they can still participate in possible upside gains. Traders should, however, be aware of potential adverse risks and make sure they are happy with the strategy's risk-return profile, especially in highly volatile industries like technology.

In the healthcare industry, using protective puts is another industry-specific option strategy. The healthcare industry is sometimes viewed as defensive because of its ability to withstand economic downturns and the steady demand for healthcare services and products. To shield themselves from any downside risk, traders can acquire protective put options at the same time as shares in healthcare companies, by enabling traders to sell their shares at a fixed price (the striking price) if the stock price drops below a specific threshold, protective puts offer downside protection. With this method, traders can still benefit from possible gains while reducing losses in unfavorable market fluctuations.

Traders may use diagonal spreads in the energy industry as a sector-specific options strategy. Commodity pricing, supply and demand dynamics, and geopolitical events significantly impact the energy sector. With diagonal spreads, traders can profit from anticipated changes in the energy sector's price or volatility. By buying a longer-term option and selling a shorter-term option with a different strike price, traders can profit from both time decay and directional fluctuations in the underlying asset. This strategy is known as a diagonal spread. Given the volatility and unpredictability of price swings in the energy industry, this method can succeed.

Calendar spreads are another tool available to traders in the consumer discretionary market. Changes in consumer attitude, the state of the economy, and spending habits all impact the consumer discretionary sector. Calendar spreads are useful for traders looking to profit on shifts in the consumer discretionary sector's anticipated volatility or mood. A calendar spread is when an option with a longer expiration date is bought and an option with a shorter expiration date is sold at the same strike price. With this technique, traders can minimize their downside risk while profiting from volatility and time decay fluctuations.

Options methods tailored to a particular industry allow traders to profit from the distinct features and dynamics of several economic sectors. Traders can improve trading performance, reduce risk, and seize profit possibilities by customizing options trading strategies to specific industries. Sector-specific options strategies enable traders to maximize their chances of success in today's dynamic and interconnected financial markets by adapting to changing market conditions. Examples of these strategies include using calendar spreads in the consumer discretionary sector, diagonal spreads in the energy sector, covered calls in the technology sector, and protective puts in the healthcare sector.

A sector-specific options strategy is a useful tool for traders looking to profit from the distinct features and dynamics of several economic sectors. Different sectors display different volatility patterns, underlying factors, and market emotions. This gives traders the chance to apply focused options trading strategies to maximize trading efficiency and reduce risk.

In the technology industry, one of the most popular industry-specific options strategies is the covered call strategy. Because of its volatility and great growth potential, the technology sector is a popular choice for covered call strategies. To make extra money, traders can buy shares of technological companies with promising futures and sell covered call options against their holdings at the same time. Traders can earn from the premium gained by selling covered calls, and if the stock price rises, they can still participate in possible upside gains. But traders need to be aware of possible negative risks, especially in industries with high volatility like technology, and make sure they are happy with the strategy's risk-return profile.

In the healthcare industry, using protective puts is another industry-specific options strategy. Because of its ability to withstand economic downturns and the steady demand for healthcare services and products, the healthcare industry is sometimes viewed as defensive. In order to shield themselves from any downside risk, traders can acquire protective put options at the same time as shares in healthcare companies. By enabling traders to sell their shares at a fixed price (the striking price) in the event that the stock price drops below a specific threshold, protective puts offer downside protection. With this method, traders can still benefit from possible gains while reducing losses in the event of unfavorable market fluctuations.

Traders may use diagonal spreads as a sector-specific options strategy in the energy industry. Commodity pricing, supply and demand dynamics, and geopolitical events all have a significant impact on the energy sector. With diagonal spreads, traders can profit from anticipated changes in the energy sector's price or volatility. By buying a longer-term option and selling a shorter-term option with a different strike price, traders can profit from both time decay and directional fluctuations in the underlying asset. This strategy is known as a diagonal spread. Given the volatility and unpredictability of price swings in the energy industry, this method can be very successful there.

Calendar spreads are another tool available to traders in the consumer discretionary market. Changes in consumer attitude, the state of the economy, and spending habits all have an impact on the consumer discretionary sector. Calendar spreads are a useful tool for traders looking to profit on shifts in the consumer discretionary sector's anticipated volatility or mood. A calendar spread is when an option with a longer expiration date is bought and an option with a shorter expiration date is sold at the same strike price. With this technique, traders can minimize their downside risk while profiting from fluctuations in volatility and time decay.

Finally, traders have the opportunity to profit from the distinct features and dynamics of various economic sectors by utilizing sector-specific options methods. Traders can improve trading performance, reduce risk, and seize profit possibilities by customizing options trading strategies to certain industries. Sector-specific options strategies enable traders to maximize their chances of success in today's dynamic and interconnected financial markets by adapting to changing market conditions. Examples of these strategies include using calendar spreads in the consumer discretionary sector,diagonal spreads in the energy sector, covered calls in the technology sector, and protective puts in the healthcare sector.

Building a sustainable trading career

A sustainable trading career takes a blend of talent, perseverance, discipline, and lifelong learning. Trading has the potential to yield significant gains, However, it also entails risks and challenges that can fool even the most experienced traders. To create a long-lasting trading career, traders need to concentrate on building a solid knowledge and skill base, implementing disciplined trading procedures, efficiently managing risk, and keeping an eye on the big picture.

Developing knowledge and abilities is one of the central tenets of creating a long-lasting trading profession. It takes time and effort for traders to learn about financial markets, trading tactics, risk management approaches, technical and fundamental analysis, and trading psychology. This could entail reading books, going to lectures and workshops, enrolling in online courses, and asking mentors and seasoned traders for advice. Traders may make better decisions and handle the challenges of trading with competence and confidence by developing a thorough awareness of the markets and trading concepts. Another crucial component of developing a long-lasting trading career is discipline. Prosperous traders maintain a structured trading strategy and continuously abide by set norms and regulations. This entails establishing precise trading goals, specifying entry and exit requirements, controlling position sizes, putting risk management plans into action, and abiding by trading norms and procedures. By exercising discipline in their trading, traders can steer clear of costly blunders, impulsive trading behavior, and emotional decision-making that could endanger their trading capital and long-term profitability.

It takes effective risk management to develop a trading profession that lasts. To safeguard their trading capital and maintain profitability over the long run, traders need to carefully evaluate and manage the risk they are exposed to. Setting risk limits, utilizing stop-loss orders, diversifying across several asset classes and strategies, and staying away from excessive leverage are all part of this. Effective risk management allows traders to reduce the effect of losses, protect capital during drawdowns, and continue to make a living from trading even in difficult market circumstances.

Developing a long-term trading profession requires keeping an eye on the broader picture. Trading is a marathon, not a sprint, and it frequently takes patience, tenacity, and fortitude to succeed in the face of difficulty. Acknowledging that losses and setbacks are an unavoidable aspect of trading, traders should concentrate on drawing lessons from their mistakes, modifying their approach, and making steady progress over time. Traders may weather short-term swings, remain steadfast in their objectives, and create a long-lasting trading career by keeping a long-term view.

Building a sustainable trading profession also requires constant learning and adaptation. Because of the dynamic and ever-evolving nature of the financial markets, traders must keep up with industry changes, new trends, and changing trading tactics. Traders need to be willing to take lessons from their past, keep up of industry advancements, and modify their trading strategy in response to shifting market conditions. To improve their abilities and methods, this may entail trying out novel approaches, utilizing cutting-edge equipment and tools, and getting input from mentors and peers

.

In summary, developing a long-term trading career necessitates a blend of expertise, self-control, risk mitigation, endurance, and ongoing education. A trading career can be sustained by traders by emphasizing the development of a strong skill base, following disciplined trading procedures, efficiently managing risk, keeping an eye on the big picture, and remaining informed about market trends. Even though the road to success could be difficult and paved with setbacks, traders who are persistent in their pursuit of excellence and committed to ongoing development can succeed in the fast-paced, fiercely competitive world of trading.

Establishing a long-term trading profession is a path that calls for tenacity, commitment to continuous progress, and dedication. The route to success in trading is often filled with obstacles and disappointments, despite the allure of the potential benefits. In order to succeed in the cutthroat world of trading and create a long-lasting career, traders must acquire a variety of skills, implement disciplined trading procedures, efficiently manage risk, keep an eye on the big picture, and place a high value on lifelong learning and adaptability.

A successful trading career is predicated on the acquisition of knowledge and abilities. It takes time and effort for traders to become knowledgeable about financial markets, trading tactics, risk management approaches, technical and fundamental analysis, and trading psychology. This could entail learning about economic indicators, investigating market dynamics, evaluating historical pricing data, and comprehending the fundamentals of behavioral finance. Traders can create strategies that are more in line with their goals and risk tolerance and make better selections by developing a thorough understanding of the markets and trading principles.

One essential component of effective trading is discipline. Maintaining a clearly defined trading plan and continuously abiding by set rules and norms are aspects of discipline. This entails establishing precise trading goals, specifying entry and exit requirements, controlling position sizes, putting risk management plans into action, and abiding by trading norms and procedures. By exercising discipline in their trading, traders can steer clear of costly blunders, impulsive trading behavior, and emotional decision-making that could endanger their trading capital and long-term profitability.

Long-term trading performance and capital preservation depend on effective risk management. To safeguard their trading capital and maintain profitability over the long run, traders need to carefully evaluate and manage the risk they are exposed to. Setting risk limits, utilizing stop-loss orders, diversifying across several asset classes and strategies, and staying away from excessive leverage are all part of this. Effective risk management allows traders to reduce the effect of losses, protect capital during drawdowns, and continue to make a living from trading even in difficult market circumstances.

In order to effectively traverse the highs and lows of trade and attain long-term, sustainable success, one must maintain a long-term perspective. Trading is a marathon, not a sprint, and it frequently takes patience, tenacity, and fortitude to succeed in the face of difficulty. Acknowledging that losses and setbacks are an unavoidable aspect of trading, traders should concentrate on drawing lessons from their mistakes, modifying their approach, and making steady progress over time. Traders may weather short-term swings, remain steadfast in their objectives, and create a long-lasting trading career by keeping a long-term view.

To survive and remain competitive in the fast-paced world of trading, one must constantly learn and adapt. Technology, laws, the state of the economy, and investor behavior are the main forces behind the ongoing evolution of the financial markets. To be current and successful in their trading attempts, traders need to keep up with market developments, new trends, and changing trading tactics. This could entail reading trading books and articles, participating in webinars, workshops, and seminars, as well as exchanging thoughts and insights with other traders and business experts. Traders may remain ahead of the curve and put themselves up for success in the dynamic world of trading by adopting a mindset of constant learning and adaptability.

In summary, developing a long-term trading career necessitates a blend of expertise, self-control, risk mitigation, endurance, and ongoing education. A trading career can be sustained and one's chances of success increased by traders who prioritize ongoing education and adaptation, stick to disciplined trading procedures, manage risk well, keep an eye on the big picture, and have a strong foundation of abilities. Even though the road may be difficult and paved with setbacks, traders who stick to their objectives and pursue ongoing development can succeed in the fast-paced, cutthroat world of trading and reach their full potential.

Adapting strategies to changing markets

For traders looking to sustain profits and successfully negotiate the complex and always changing world of financial markets, the ability to modify strategy in response to shifting market conditions is essential. Numerous factors, such as economic statistics, geopolitical developments, technology improvements, and changes in investor attitude, constantly impact market circumstances. Consequently, trading tactics that worked well in one market context might not work as well or even be harmful in another. In order to thrive in dynamic markets, traders need to maintain a flexible, proactive, and adaptive trading style.

Recognizing changes in market dynamics and spotting new trends or patterns is essential to adjusting strategy to shifting markets. In addition to keeping a close eye on market conditions, traders also need to study price action, volume, and volatility patterns as well as keep up with pertinent news and events that could affect mood in the market and asset values. Traders can take advantage of fresh possibilities and reduce risks under dynamic market conditions by being alert and perceptive enough to recognize shifts in market behavior and modify their trading methods accordingly.

Being adaptable is crucial when modifying strategy to fit shifting market conditions. It is imperative for traders to exhibit flexibility in altering or completely giving up on methods that no longer correspond with the state of the market or do not yield profitable results. To better fit the current market situation, this may entail modifying factors like entry and exit criteria, position sizes, risk management strategies, or timeframes. In addition, traders might need to look at alternative asset classes or trading strategies that have better chances for profit in shifting market conditions.

Adapting tactics to shifting markets requires proactive risk management. Trading carries risks, and those risks change as the market does. In order to safeguard their trading money and maintain profitability, traders must periodically evaluate their risk exposure, modify risk management settings as necessary, and put strategies into place. This could entail employing options or other derivative instruments to hedge against possible losses, tightening stop-loss orders, decreasing position sizes, and improving diversification. Effective risk management enables traders to respond resiliently and with confidence to shifting market conditions.

Keeping up with new advances in trading technologies, tools, and procedures is another crucial component of adjusting strategies to shifting markets. Technological developments have completely changed how traders evaluate market data, place orders, and control risk. In order to remain competitive in today's data-driven and fast-paced markets, traders need to embrace new technology and integrate them into their trading toolkit. To obtain insights, spot opportunities, and execute trades more quickly, this may entail utilizing machine learning algorithms, automated trading platforms, enhanced charting tools, or algorithmic trading systems.

Additionally, traders need to maintain an open-minded and flexible mindset when it comes to trading. Because of the sudden and quick changes in the market, traders must be quick to adapt and change their plans of action. This could entail acting quickly in reaction to unanticipated events that affect asset values and market sentiment, abrupt changes in price, or breaking news. To seize fresh possibilities and adjust to shifting market dynamics as they present themselves, traders need to be ready to pivot or alter course as necessary.

For traders hoping to stay profitable and thrive in the competitive and dynamic financial markets of today, it is imperative that they modify their strategy in response to shifting market conditions. Trades can be resilient and confident in their ability to handle shifting market situations by remaining alert, flexible, proactive, and adaptive. In the face of shifting market conditions, by recognizing shifts in the market dynamics, adjusting their trading tactics, implementing proactive risk management, embracing new technologies, or remaining flexible and

open-minded, trading professionals can raise their odds of success and fulfill their trading goals.

A thorough grasp of investor behavior and market psychology is necessary to modify plans in response to shifting market conditions. To effectively assess the mood of market participants, traders need to read market sentiment and sentiment indicators in addition to technical indications and chart patterns. Sentiment indicators that might assist traders predict future market reversals or trend continuations include the put/call ratio, the volatility index (VIX), and investor surveys. These indicators offer insightful information about the mood of the market. Traders can more effectively adjust to shifting market conditions and make more knowledgeable trading selections by using sentiment analysis into their trading techniques.

In addition, macroeconomic variables and geopolitical developments have a big impact on asset values and market patterns. To evaluate the state of the economy and foresee future changes in market sentiment, traders need to keep an eye on economic indicators like GDP growth, inflation rates, interest rates, and unemployment statistics. Furthermore, market volatility and investor confidence can be significantly impacted by geopolitical events including trade disputes, geopolitical tensions, and geopolitical conflicts. Traders need to keep up with geopolitical developments and evaluate how they might affect the financial markets in order to modify their trading strategy.

As plans are modified to accommodate shifting markets, risk management is still crucial. Trading carries risks, and those risks change as the market does. In order to safeguard their trading capital and maintain profitability in the face of fluctuating market conditions, traders need to implement strong risk management procedures. This could entail employing stop-loss orders, limiting risk, diversifying investments, and using options or other derivative instruments to hedge against possible losses. Traders may confidently handle shifting market conditions and lessen the impact of unfavorable market moves by practicing competent risk management.

Furthermore, it is crucial to keep a disciplined approach to trading when modifying methods in response to shifting market conditions. Even in the midst of market volatility or uncertainty, traders need to stay true to their trading plans and methods. Fear, greed, and overconfidence are a few examples of emotions that can impair judgment and cause traders to act impulsively, deviating from their original trading plan. Regardless of shifting market conditions, traders may be disciplined and adhere to predetermined trading rules and risk restrictions, which will help them avoid costly blunders and preserve consistency in their trading performance.

Trading professionals who want to successfully modify their methods in response to shifting markets must also prioritize lifelong learning and personal development. Because of the dynamic and ever-changing nature of the financial markets, traders must keep up with the latest innovations, fashions, and strategies. Traders should make an investment in their education by reading books and articles on trading, participating in workshops, webinars, and seminars, as well as by exchanging thoughts and insights with other traders and professionals in the sector. It is possible for traders to raise their overall trading performance and their flexibility and agility in responding to shifting market conditions by consistently broadening their knowledge and skill set.

Finally, it should be noted that adjusting strategies to shifting markets is a complex process that calls for alertness, adaptability, proactive risk management, discipline, ongoing learning, and self-improvement. Through the use of sentiment analysis, keeping an eye on geopolitical and macroeconomic trends, putting strong risk management procedures in place, remaining disciplined, and investing in ongoing education, traders can successfully adjust their strategies to shifting market conditions and raise their prospects of success in the ruthless, quick-paced financial markets of today.

Understanding regulations and ethical considerations

Traders in financial markets need to know about rules and ethical issues in order to follow the law, be honest, and follow ethical standards. There are a lot of rules and regulations that control the financial markets. These are meant to make them fair, transparent, and protect investors. These rules cover many different areas, such as securities laws, rules for keeping the market honest, rules against laundering money, and steps to protect investors. Traders need to know the rules that apply to them and ensure that their trading actions are legal so that they don't get fined, punished, or have other legal problems.

A critical part of knowing regulations is keeping up with changes and new versions of regulations. Financial rules are constantly changing to keep up with new technologies, changes in how markets work, and new risks. The Securities and Exchange Commission, the Commodity Futures Trading Commission, the Financial Industry Regulatory Authority, and other pertinent regulatory organizations have new rules, modifications, and enforcement actions that traders need to be aware of. Attending regulatory training events, subscribing to regulatory newsletters, or speaking with attorneys are some ways to stay informed about changes to regulatory standards and make sure they are being followed.

Concerns about ethics are also significant in dealing, because traders must follow ethical rules and principles to keep the markets honest and trustworthy. Many things fall under the ethics category, such as being honest, fair, open, private, and avoiding conflicts of interest. Traders should be truthful and not do anything unethical, like trading on inside knowledge, manipulating the market, jumping the gun, or giving false information. Not only does following ethical rules help build trust in the financial markets, but it also helps traders build a good name and respect in the field.

Another important social thing to think about when trading is transparency. Traders should try to be honest with clients, other traders, and regulatory officials about their trading activities, investment strategies, and any possible conflicts of interest. They should give accurate and up-to-date information about these things. Transparency builds belief in the fairness of the financial markets and keeps people from misinterpreting information, arguing, or accusing others of wrongdoing. Traders should keep detailed records of all the trades, contacts, and activities they do to show that they are honest and responsible in their dealings.

Traders also need to think about how their actions will affect other people in the market and the business as a whole. Traders' actions can have big effects on the market's liquidity, price stability, and investor trust. Trading people should know what their duties are as market players and behave in a way that supports the fairness and smooth running of financial markets. This could mean avoiding too much speculation, boosting market integrity, and making the market more liquid and efficient.

Following the rules and being ethical is not only the law, but also the right thing to do as a worker and with integrity. In their interactions with customers, counterparties, and regulatory authorities, traders must act in a way that upholds the ideals of fairness, transparency, and trustworthiness. By knowing the rules and ethical issues that come up, traders can make sure they follow the law, stay honest, and follow ethical standards in their trading. In addition to keeping investors and market players safe, this also helps keep financial markets honest and stable as a whole.

For traders in the financial markets, understanding the rules and ethical issues is very important because it's the basis for responsible and long-lasting dealing. Market participants and brokerage companies can avoid legal trouble by following the rules set by regulators. These rules also help keep the markets honest and fair. The complicated web of rules that guide financial markets includes many different areas, from laws against securities fraud to rules against money laundering. These rules are all meant to protect investors and keep the market stable.

Traders need to keep up with changes and updates to regulations in order to stay in line with changing legal requirements. Regulatory bodies like the SEC, CFTC, and FINRA often issue new rules, changes to old ones, and enforcement steps in response to new risks and changes in the market. Traders must actively participate in regulatory training events, subscribe to regulatory newsletters, and get legal advice in order to stay up to date on regulatory changes and make sure they are following all laws.

Along with following the rules, traders' actions and behavior in financial markets are largely determined by their morals. To keep trust and integrity in financial deals, it's important to follow ethical principles like being honest, fair, open, and private. Traders should not do anything unethical, like insider trading, market manipulation, or giving false information about what they know. These actions not only break ethical rules, but they also hurt market integrity and trust.

Another important part of ethical dealing is being open and honest. Traders should try to give clients, counterparties, and regulatory authorities accurate and up-to-date information about their trading actions, investment strategies, and any possible conflicts of interest. Transparency builds belief in the fairness of the financial markets and keeps people from misinterpreting information, arguing, or accusing others of wrongdoing. Trading activities and contacts should be recorded in great detail so that traders are more open and accountable in their dealings.

Traders also need to think about how their actions affect other people in the market and the business as a whole. Traders must always be responsible and do what's best for the market because their actions can affect market liquidity, price stability, and investor trust. Traders can help keep the financial ecosystem healthy and strong by avoiding too much speculation, boosting market integrity, and making the market more liquid and efficient.

Following rules and morals is more than just the law's requirement; it shows that traders are dedicated to industry, honesty, and responsible behavior in the financial markets. Traders protect investors and market players by following the rules set by regulators, acting in an honest way, and encouraging openness and responsibility in their business. They also help keep the financial markets stable and honest as a whole.

Understanding and following the rules and thinking about what is right are the most important parts of dealing in a way that is both sustainable and moral.

Ensuring compliance in options trading

Maintaining market integrity, safeguarding investor interests, and adhering to regulatory requirements depend upon traders and brokerage firms maintaining compliance in options trading. A thorough regulatory framework governing options trading has been built by various regulatory bodies and regulatory agencies, including the Financial Industry Regulatory Authority, Commodity Futures Trading Commission, Securities and Exchange Commission, and others. Adherence to these standards serves as a deterrent against illicit acts that can potentially compromise market stability and erode investor trust, such as insider trading, fraud, and market manipulation.

Following the disclosure rules is one of the most essential parts of ensuring that options trading is compliant. Investors need accurate and timely information on the costs, risks, and potential benefits of options trading from traders and brokerage firms. This involves revealing the dangers of trading options, like leverage, volatility, and principle loss possibilities. In addition, traders are required to educate clients about their investing goals, trading tactics, and any potential conflicts of interest that can surface during client interactions.

Another crucial component of guaranteeing compliance in options trading is risk management. In order to safeguard investors' funds and reduce the chance of loss, traders and brokerage firms need to put strong risk management procedures in place. To detect and reduce possible risks, this may entail diversifying portfolios, putting stop-loss orders into place, setting risk limits, and regularly monitoring positions. Traders and brokerage firms can safeguard investors' capital and guarantee regulatory compliance by proficiently managing risk.

In the realm of options trading, adherence to laws and regulations is equally crucial. The specified trading standards, which include margin requirements, position limits, order execution requirements, and reporting obligations, must be followed by traders and brokerage firms. This include following regulations on margin trading and leverage, guaranteeing optimal execution, and carrying out customer orders in a timely and precise manner. To preserve openness and accountability in the market, traders and brokerage firms must also promptly and accurately report trading activities to regulatory bodies.

Moreover, brokerage houses must establish strong internal controls and monitoring methods to guarantee compliance in options trading. Brokerage companies are required to set up policies and procedures to oversee and monitor the trading of options, identify possible regulatory or internal policy infractions, and take the necessary corrective action. To verify compliance with internal policies and legal requirements, this may entail doing routine audits, reviews, and compliance assessments. Brokerage businesses can assist in preventing misbehavior and fostering a compliance culture inside the company by putting in place efficient internal controls and monitoring systems.

Another crucial element in guaranteeing compliance in options trading is education and training. Adequate training and instruction on options trading regulations, compliance requirements, and ethical standards must be provided to traders and brokerage business personnel. This entails being aware of the legal and regulatory environment surrounding the trading of options, recognizing possible compliance risks, and being competent in handling compliance-related concerns. Brokerage companies may enable their staff to make knowledgeable judgments, follow rules and regulations, and by offering instruction and training, in accordance with applicable rules and regulations.

Maintaining market integrity, safeguarding investor interests, and adhering to regulatory regulations all depend on options traders making sure they are in compliance. Adherence to disclosure mandates, risk mitigation strategies, trading protocols, internal controls, and oversight systems serves as a safeguard against fraudulent operations, market manipulation, and other illicit actions that pose a threat to investor welfare and compromise market stability. Traders and brokerage firms can protect investors' funds, promote a culture of compliance, and guarantee the integrity and transparency of the options trading markets by following regulatory regulations, putting in place strong internal controls, and funding training and education programs.

Apart from the fundamental elements mentioned, continuous observation and adjustment to regulatory modifications and market advancements are necessary to guarantee compliance in the options trading industry. Regulations can alter over time in reaction to new hazards that arise, new developments in technology, and shifts in the market. To guarantee ongoing compliance with relevant laws and regulations, traders and brokerage firms must keep up with regulatory developments, guidance, and enforcement actions issued by regulatory agencies.

To stay up to date on changes in regulatory standards and industry best practices, this calls for proactive contact with regulatory agencies, involvement in industry forums and working groups, and cooperation with legal and compliance specialists. Traders and brokerage firms can successfully manage compliance risks and reflect changing regulatory expectations by being proactive and involved with regulatory developments. This allows them to modify their compliance processes and procedures.

Furthermore, cultivating an ethical and honest culture inside the company is essential to guaranteeing compliance in the trading of options. Maintaining market confidence and trust in financial markets is largely dependent on ethical issues. Integrity and ethical behavior must be encouraged by traders and brokerage firms in their interactions with counterparties, clients, and regulatory bodies. This entails encouraging an environment of openness, truthfulness, and justice as well as holding staff members responsible for maintaining moral principles and following legal obligations.

Brokerage companies can create policies and procedures that highlight the value of moral behavior and following rules in order to foster a culture of ethics and compliance. This can entail putting codes of conduct into place, holding ethics education and awareness campaigns, and setting up channels via which staff members can discreetly report any potential infractions of the law or ethical issues. Brokerage companies can build trust and confidence in the honesty of their operations and improve their standing in the market by encouraging a culture of ethics and compliance.

Furthermore, coordination and cooperation between market players, regulatory bodies, and industry stakeholders are necessary to ensure compliance in options trading. In order to successfully address compliance issues, respond to regulatory investigations, and implement regulatory reforms, traders and brokerage firms must collaborate with regulatory authorities. To support efficient regulation and market integrity, this may entail taking part in regulatory consultations, offering input on draft regulations, and exchanging best practices with peers in the sector and regulators.

In summary, maintaining compliance in the options trading sector is a complex process that calls for constant attention, flexibility, and cooperation from traders, brokerage houses, government agencies, and other industry participants. Maintaining market integrity, safeguarding investor interests, and preserving faith and confidence in financial markets all depend on adherence to legal obligations, moral principles, and industry best practices. Traders and brokerage firms can guarantee ongoing regulatory compliance and advance an equitable, transparent, and effective options trading market by remaining proactive, cultivating a culture of ethics and compliance, and working with regulatory bodies and industry stakeholders.

CONCLUSION

"Options Odyssey: Navigating the World of Trading Strategies" serves as a comprehensive roadmap for traders of all levels, empowering them to unlock opportunities in the stock market through the dynamic realm of options trading. Throughout this journey, readers have delved into the intricacies of various trading strategies, gaining valuable insights, practical techniques, and expert guidance to navigate the complexities of options markets with confidence and precision. From understanding the fundamentals to mastering advanced strategies, this book has equipped traders with the knowledge and skills necessary to thrive in today's fast-paced financial landscape. With clear explanations, real-world examples, and actionable tips, "Options Odyssey" has provided readers with the tools they need to enhance their trading performance, manage risk effectively, and achieve their financial goals. As readers embark on their options odyssey, they are poised to unlock the potential for unlimited opportunities in the stock market and embark on a path to long-term success in trading.

Thank you for buying and reading/ listening to our book. If you found this book useful/ helpful please take a few minutes and leave a review on the platform where you purchased our book. Your feedback matters greatly to us.